Grace to you.

10 STEPS
Toward a
Better Life

10 STEPS
Toward a Better Life

David C. Cooper

Foreword by Ron Blue

Pathway
PRESS

Book Editor: Wanda Griffith
Editorial Assistant: Tammy Hatfield
Copy Editors: Esther Metaxas
Aimee Norton

Library of Congress Catalog Card Number: 2004097988
ISBN: 1-59684-026-9
Copyright © 2005 by Pathway Press
Cleveland, Tennessee 37311
All Rights Reserved
Printed in the United States of America

DEDICATION

To my beautiful and graceful wife,

Barbie,

whose faith and faithfulness
give me strength for life's journey.

CONTENTS

FOREWORD

Dr. Cooper has written a book that has the potential to be used by the Holy Spirit to change your life. On the second page he says, "You need a mission statement that governs your life. Every day needs to be lived with purpose." If we stopped right there and asked what is it that governs our lives, we have some real soul-searching to do. Today's culture attempts to govern our lives by enticing us to self-satisfaction and self-glorification.

What a great question, "What is it that governs my life?" If, at the end of each day, I ask myself, "Did I live today on purpose, with purpose?" I know that at the end of my life I will be able to hear my Master say, "Well done, good and faithful servant." This is just the beginning.

After committing my life to Christ in 1972, five years later I committed my life to full-time ministry. I have been married 40 years and have had the privilege, by living this long, of reading many great books written by great authors. I have had the opportunity to hear many great speakers, but one of the greatest privileges I have had over the last several years is for my wife, Judy, and me to sit under the teaching and leadership of Dr. Cooper. Not a Sunday goes by that we are not profoundly impacted. We look forward with great anticipation to every worship service and regret those times we have to miss. Dr. Cooper's teaching comes from a deep spiritual understanding of God's Word—always presented with humor, illustrations, and in every case applicable. I leave each service with pages of notes that challenge and encourage me throughout the week.

The one trait I admire most in great leaders is that they "walk their talk." Dr. Cooper walks his talk, and this book is a part of his walk. *Ten Steps Toward a Better Life* begins with excellence and ends in my area of expertise, financial freedom. Because I have had the privilege of writing and speaking on this topic myself for many years, I was once again challenged about what God has to say relative to our finances.

As I look through the Table of Contents, I am reminded of how I desire to achieve excellence, walk with spiritual maturity, live by faith, experience perfect peace, and know that God's wisdom transcends time, cultures and my experiences. I look for what true success is, desire healthy relationships, have a tremendous desire to have a powerful prayer life, make dynamic decisions, and, of course, live with financial freedom. I can guarantee you that if you read this book prayerfully and meditatively, your life will certainly be changed.

This book illustrates to me Dr. Cooper's ministry. Filled with illustrations, humor, scriptures and next steps, every chapter, by itself, can lead to a life-changing experience. It is Biblical, practical and, most importantly, from a reader's standpoint, very readable. I trust that you will enjoy this book and that it will become an ongoing reference to you in your spiritual life.

—Ron Blue
Christian Financial Professionals Network

Achieving Excellence

Isaac D'Israel said: "It is a wretched taste to be gratified with mediocrity when the excellent lies before us."

Excellence is the master key to success in any endeavor. *Excellence* means "the very best quality; superiority; first-rate; exceptionally good." Edwin Bliss once said, "The pursuit of excellence is gratifying and healthy. The pursuit of perfection is frustrating, neurotic, and a terrible waste of time."[1]

Booker T. Washington said, "Excellence is to do a common thing in an uncommon way." There is no room for status quo and mediocrity in the kingdom of God. God created us for excellence. Christ deserves our excellence. The Holy Spirit empowers us for excellence. The times require excellence.

You are "fearfully and wonderfully made" by the Creator and you are "crowned with glory and honor" with an infinite resource of potential (see Psalms 8:4-7; 139:14). You were made for greatness.

Excellence requires us to mix hard work and diligence with the potential God has given us. Talent and abilities are not enough. "Make every effort to add to your faith" (2 Peter 1:5). Success doesn't come from simply making an effort but by making every effort.

Texans are known for having a penchant for excellence. They're known for having the biggest and best of everything. A Texas rancher vacationed in Australia. He met a farmer who liked to show off his wheat fields. "We've got wheat fields twice as big back home," said the Texan.

As they walked along, the Aussie showed the Texan his heads of cattle. "We've got Longhorns that are twice as big," bragged the Texan. About that time two kangaroo came bouncing across the field.

Startled, the Texan said, "Good heavens, what are those?"

Said the Aussie, "Aintcha got grasshoppers in Texas?"

This is the standard of excellence: "Whatever you do, work at it with all your heart as working for the Lord not for men" (Colossians 3:23). Here are 10 principles for achieving a life of excellence.

#1 MISSION

You need a mission statement that governs your life. Every day needs to be lived with purpose. After President Ronald Reagan died, a political commentator noted that while his polices are debated, the one thing he did right was focus on the "big ideas." His big ideas of putting America back to work after the deep recession of the '70s and of ending the cold war were the right ideas, and he stuck to them.

We need to keep the big picture in mind and not get lost in trivial details. Our mission statement must begin with our spiritual commitment. Jesus gave us a master mission for life and for the church: "Go . . .

make disciples of all nations" (Matthew 28:19). In everything we do in life, marriage, career, raising children, managing money . . . we are to make disciples.

#2 MASTER PLAN

Don't drift with the tide. Get a master plan for your life. Set concrete goals and develop a workable strategy to reach them. When you build a house, you start with a master site plan and then work to complete the plan—making adjustments as you go. Can you imagine the chaos that would occur by trying to build a house without a set of blueprints?

Jesus talked about the need to sit down and count the cost before we start to build, to see if we have the needed resources to finish (see Luke 14:28-30). Without a master site plan, we react to one situation after another. Circumstances and emergencies plan our agenda, instead of setting our own agenda and then working the plan.

When I went to college, my goal was to receive a doctorate, not a bachelor's degree. So the bachelor's degree was just a step is a larger master plan. Then I got my master's degree in counseling. While it brought me a great sense of accomplishment, I was still only two-thirds of the way to the finish line. When I graduated with my doctorate, my goal was reached.

Here are the two questions to give you direction in life: Where do you want to go? How do you plan to get there? Ask these questions about every major decision you face, and you find your way clearly to reach your goals.

#3 MANAGEMENT

Life won't fly on auto pilot. Neither will a marriage, a career, a business, a ministry or anything. Pay attention to details. Why do businesses go bankrupt? A study revealed that businesses go bankrupt because of poor quality service and the failure to pay attention to details.

While we need to focus on the big picture, remember that the big picture is simply a collection of details. As Solomon reminds us, "The little foxes . . . spoil the vine" (Song of Solomon 2:15, *NKJV*).

Management means quality control. In America, we often think that bigger is better. But bigger is not always better—it's just more stressful. We need to focus on quality in our life, work and ministry, and let God control the quantity.

- Don't try to build a bigger business—build a better business and it will grow bigger.

- Don't worry about making more money—focus on managing your money better and your net worth will grow.

- Don't ask for more time to do a project—use the time you have in a more efficient manner.

- Don't chase a bigger dream—chase a better dream!

Excellence means quality control in every area of life. A commitment to quality is a mark of high self-esteem. People who care about the quality of their work, care about themselves. No one has known the power of quality any more than Antonio Stradivari, the Italian violin maker (1644 to 1737). He lived to be 93 years old in a time when the average life expectancy was a little over 30. Self-taught, he worked alone with simple tools until his sons joined him in business late in his life. When Stradivari finished a violin, and it passed his high standards of excellence, he signed it. Today, a Stradivarius violin sells for thousands of dollars because his name is synonymous with excellence.

#4 MODELS

Role models are vital in helping us achieve our best. "As iron sharpens iron, so one man sharpens another" (Proverbs 27:17). We need iron in our relationships that can test us and sharpen us. We shouldn't surround ourselves with soft people who comply with our every request. Immature people don't have enough "iron" in their lives, while mature people have true mentors and peers who test them.

We need to seek out models like the young prophet Elisha sought Elijah, the seasoned man of God. We can't expect a mentor to come looking for us. We must take the initiative and seek out wise counselors and seasoned leaders.

The concept of competition is distorted in our times. Real competition means to compete against a winner so as to bring out the winner in us. We aren't trying to defeat an opponent in a triumphant sense, but in a sense to reach our highest potential. We need relationships of tension to reach excellence. In the end, we are only competing against ourselves; against our desires, disciplines and habits.

I run every day for exercise. When I run, I am often surrounded by other runners. I don't try to run at their pace; I'm not competing against them. I am competing against my inner resolve to push myself toward the goal. However, when I get around a faster runner, it helps me push myself toward my ultimate potential.

#5 MAINTENANCE

Most products today come with a maintenance plan or one the sales person will offer. Some plans are absurd, like the $100 plan for a $75 CD player!

Paul talks to Timothy, his protégé, about his personal maintenance plan (1 Timothy 4:7, 8). What is our routine to stay in shape mentally, physically, emotionally and spiritually? We either develop, or we deteriorate. Success requires discipline, and discipline means routine habits. Here's a reminder of the power of habit.

> *You may know me.*
> *I'm your constant companion.*
> *I'm your greatest helper, I'm your heaviest burden.*
> *I will push you onward or drag you down to failure.*
> *I am at your command.*
> *Half the tasks you do might as well be turned over to me.*
> *I'm able to do them quickly and I'm able to do them the same every time if that's what you want.*
> *I'm easily managed; all you've got to do is be firm with me.*
> *Show me exactly how you want it done. After a few lessons, I'll do it automatically.*
> *I am the servant of all great men and women; of course, servant of the failures as well.*

*I've made all great individuals who have ever been
    great.*
And I've made all the failures, too.
*But I work with all the precision of a marvelous com-
    puter with the intelligence of a human being.*
*You may run me from profit or you may run me to
    ruin, it makes no difference to me.*
Take me. Be easy with me, and I will destroy you.
Be firm with me, and I'll put the world at your feet.
Who am I?
I am Habit!

—Author Unknown

#6 MIRROR

The apostle Paul said, "Examine yourself . . . test yourself" (see 2 Corinthians 13:5). Plato said "The unexamined life is not worth living."

When you look in the mirror at work, are you proud of the person you see? Take time to examine yourself in light of the person of Christ himself. What is the image of Christ in you?

Paul tells us clearly that "The fruit of the Spirit (that means the end result of what the Holy Spirit is doing in us) is love, joy, peace, patience, kindness, goodness, faithfulness, gentleness and self-control" (Galatians 5:22, 23, parenthesis added).

We need to examine ourselves in light of Scripture. The Bible is the inspired, infallible and authoritative Word of God. It is "a lamp unto [our] feet and a light unto [our] path" (Psalm 119:105, KJV). The apostle James says it is a mirror by which we evaluate our attitudes, values, beliefs and lifestyle. Consistent exposure to the Bible brings a transformation of life.

> Anyone who listens to the word but does not do
> what it says is like a man who looks at his face in
> a mirror and, after looking at himself, goes away
> and immediately forgets what he looks like. But
> the man who looks intently into the perfect law
> that gives freedom, and continues to do this, not
> forgetting what he has heard, but doing it—he
> will be blessed in what he does (James 1:23-25).

Finally, we need to evaluate ourselves in light of our best self. Ask the question: "Is this my best self?" Am I living up to my highest potential? Am I the person I want to be and that I can be?

I am sure we all are aware of our weaknesses—probably more than we are our strengths. No one is perfect, but we also know when we are falling short of the standards and goals we have set. When we do, we need to get back on track and live up to our potential. "Live a life worthy of the calling you have received" (Ephesians 4:1).

#7 MISTAKES

This statement in the Bible gives me great encouragement: "We all stumble in many ways" (James 3:2). I'm glad I'm not the only one who struggles with issues, fails at times and comes up short. We all do. Now, I know some people who think they are perfect, so I like to remind them that *we all stumble in many ways!*

The question is not whether or not you will fail, but do your failures and mistakes defeat you or develop you? Winston Churchill said, "Success is going from one failure to another without losing your enthusiasm."

Excellence does not mean perfection. "Life is not a spelling bee!" says Harold Kushner. Failure is never final with the grace of God.

Peter failed the Lord by denying Him and deserting Him. After the Resurrection, Peter gave up trying to be a disciple. He went back to his fishing business. But the risen Lord went to the Sea of Galilee early one morning to reclaim His fallen follower (see John 21). While they were in the boats, Jesus stood on the shore and called out to them, "Have you caught any fish?" "No," they answered.

Then came the direction they needed. Jesus said, "Throw your net in on the right side of the boat." When they did, they caught more fish than their nets could contain!

What do we learn from this inspiring story? Christ gives us two directions when we make mistakes: First, *try it again.* Jesus was using fishing as a metaphor of His commission for them to try being fishers of men after they failed.

Second, *fish on the right side of the boat.* Fish where the fish are biting! Don't beat our heads against the wall trying to fish in the wrong area. I counseled a young woman in her early 30s who had just been divorced for the second time. Exasperated with herself she said, "I don't know why I keep making the same bad decisions."

Great success stories are marked by mistakes. Did you know . . .

- Henry Ford failed to put a reverse gear in his first car.

- Thomas Edison failed in 2,000 experiments before he finally invented the light bulb.

- The first time Benjamin Disraeli, prime minister of England, spoke before Parliament, members hissed him into silence and laughed when he said, "Though I sit down now, the time will come when you will hear me."

- Abraham Lincoln lost nine elections for political office and failed in business twice before finally being elected president.

- Albert Einstein was dismissed from school because he lacked interest in his studies, failed an entrance exam to a school in Zurich and was later fired from his job as tutor.

- Beethoven's music teacher, the brilliant John Albrechtsberger, said he would never compose any worthwhile music because he failed to follow the rules of musical composition.

- In 1932 when Fred Astaire was starting out, a Hollywood talent judge wrote on his screen test: "Can't act. Can't sing. Can dance a little."

- When Bob Dylan performed at a high school talent show, his classmates booed him off the stage.

- W. Clement Stone, successful insurance company executive and founder of *Success* magazine, was a high school dropout.

- Michael Jordan failed to make the junior varsity basketball team when he tried out. Later, the school principal told him to consider enlisting in the Air Force Academy after high school, which would be his best option for a career.

- One of my favorite verses is Micah 7:8: "Do not gloat over me my enemy; though I have fallen, I will rise." Make that statement right now: "Though I have fallen, I will rise!"

#8 MOTIVATION

Jesus was the most focused and highly motivated person who ever lived. He was consumed with zeal for the house of the Lord (see John 2:17). Paul challenges us: "Never be lacking zeal, but keep your spiritual fervor, serving the Lord" (Romans 12:11).

All successful people have learned the art of self-motivation. To *motivate* means "to incite to action; to impel forward; and to stir up passion." As believers, we have the Holy Spirit who motivates us. "For it is God who works in you to will and to act according to his good purpose" (Philippians 2:13).

We also need to motivate ourselves. When David, the psalmist, hit rock bottom, and no one supported him, he "encouraged himself in the Lord his God" (1 Samuel 30:6, KJV). Sometimes we just have to encourage ourselves.

I heard T.D. Jakes tell his congregation, "I don't need you to make my dreams come true!" He certainly wanted their support, but he wasn't dependent on it. That was the point he was making. We certainly need others to help us and to encourage us, but at the end of the day, it's just God and me and that constitutes a majority. Sometimes we may have to "go it alone" and encourage ourselves until others see our vision and lend their support.

But don't give up in the lonely times. Encourage yourself in the Lord by remembering three things:

- *God is with you!*

- *God is in you!*

- *God is for you!*

#9 MODERNIZATION

Excellence means to do things better in a more efficient way. Improve the quality of your product. Discard old ways of doing things that no longer work. Avoid the trap of traditions that have seen their day. The seven last words of the church are: WE NEVER DID IT THAT WAY BEFORE.

The myth that yesterday's solutions will solve today's problems is a deathblow to organizations and relationships. We see it in stagnant marriages, unproductive businesses and lifeless congregations. Die hard traditionalists sit idly by, talking about the good ole days, while life passes them by. The only good day is today! This is the only day God has given us, so let us enjoy it and make the most of it.

Jesus taught us to get new wineskins for the new wine of God's grace (Mark 2:22). The new wineskin is a metaphor for a new way of doing things. He taught us to be careful that "God-in-the-Box" thinking does not cause us to miss what God is doing in our times because we narrowly think, "God doesn't work that way." Of his own generation He said, "You did not recognize the time of God's coming to you" (Luke 19:44). They missed out on the blessings of God because they were trapped by their traditions.

In 1968, the Swiss dominated the world market for watches, producing two out of every three watches sold. Yet, within a decade, their market share plunged to a mere seven percent— all because they clung to the assumption that electronic timepieces would never sell. They failed to modernize and lost the cutting edge of excellence.[2]

#10 MOMENTUM

In athletics, we call it the Big Mo. Jesus started a small movement and let it gain momentum, which today is still gaining more momentum. The church is the largest, fastest-growing and most-influential movement that has ever existed in the history of the world. Over a third of the world's population are devoted followers of Jesus Christ and the movement is growing so rapidly around the world that projections indicate half the world's population will be Christian within 50 years.

Many people start a project with a big bang and then fizzle out. So how do you build and keep momentum? There are three important steps:

1. *Start small.* Jesus started with only 12 disciples. Every great project begins small. Just an idea. Just a single step of faith. Just a simple act. But the process toward greatness has begun.

2. *Go deep.* Develop your foundation. Grow deep roots. Strive for stability in relationship, projects, investments, ministry and business ventures. When adversity comes, stand firm and grow even through the hard times.

3. *Think big.* Dream big dreams. Set your sights high. Small-minded people never accomplish great things, only small things. Until you can see it by faith, you can't make it happen. Jesus said the kingdom of God itself is like yeast that gradually works through the whole batch of dough. Yet when it finishes its permeating effect, the whole batch is leavened (Matthew 13:33). You see, the kingdom of God starts small, but grows big.

When Jesus commissioned His followers, He was thinking of the whole world. "Go into all the world and preach the good news to all creation," was his final challenge before ascending to heaven (Mark 16:15). That was an enormous vision and a huge challenge to that handful of original disciples. But he was able to convince them that they were capable of reaching the whole world with the good news of His salvation.

I watched a television update on the Christian revival in China. There are an estimated 80 million Christians in China today. They believe that God has called them to bring the gospel to Jerusalem. They are thinking big for world evangelism!

So, start small, go deep and think big, and your dreams will become reality!

Endnotes

[1] Tim Hansel, *Eating Problems for Breakfast* (Nashville: Word, 1988) 39.

[2] "The Blight of Bad Assumptions," *Barna Report* 1, no. 2 (1996) 6-7.

SPIRITUAL MATURITY

"All children except one, grow up." So begins the classic *Peter Pan*. We all grow up, or at least we are supposed to. How we grow mentally, emotionally, physically, socially and, most importantly, spiritually determines the quality of life we live.

Have you ever stopped to think about why Jesus described salvation as a new birth? His message was, "You must be born again." Birth, you see, is the beginning of a growth process. Just as we grow through life's seasons, we grow through spiritual seasons.

We begin our spiritual journey as infants, just like we begin our physical life. We have a simple trust like small children. Jerry Seinfeld says, "A 2-year-old is like a blender without the top on."

Then we go through spiritual adolescence, questioning everything and sometimes rebelling. We then become young adults, getting focused on God's purpose. Our productive years in life and service come after that.

Finally, we reach the final stage of influence. A reporter interviewed a 104-year-old woman: "What is the best thing about being 104?"

She replied: "No peer pressure."

We either grow or we die; we develop or we deteriorate; we advance or we retreat. To *grow* means "to increase in size, amount and degree, to come to be gradually, and to progress toward maturity." God doesn't call us to perfection—He calls us to maturity. "Let us go on to maturity" (Hebrews 6:1).

#1 GROW DOWN

Strong, deep roots determine the quality of growth. Paul says we need to be "rooted and built up . . . strengthened in the faith" (Colossians 2:7). We need deep spiritual roots of a tested-and-tried faith. Without them, the storms of life will uproot us.

We will face the storm of personal testing. Trouble is no respecter of persons. I once read that we should be kind to everyone we meet, because everyone is going through some kind of pain. But God is with us in our difficulties, failures and doubts. He will never leave us nor abandon us. A deeply rooted faith is confident in the faithfulness of God, knowing that nothing "will be able to separate us from the love of God that is in Christ Jesus our Lord" (Romans 8:39).

We also face the storm of temptation. Our deepest moral and ethical convictions will be challenged. We will be called upon to stand up for what we believe in the hour of temptation. Even Christ faced temptation in the desert, alone with the devil. He wasn't exempt, and neither are we. Here's the good news:

> No temptation has seized you except what is common to man. And God is faithful; he will not let you be tempted beyond what you can

bear. But when you are tempted, he will also provide a way out so that you can stand up under it (1 Corinthians 10:13).

We also face the storm of misguided teachings. Ours is the day of false prophets, false Christs and distorted spiritual messages. Moral and spiritual confusion is the order of the day. Pollster George Gallup Jr. notes:

> The problem is not that Americans don't believe, it's that they believe everything. Thus, we find in the extreme cases the weekly church goer who believes in everything from channeling, and the born-again Christian who believes in ghosts and witches. The question is how can churches help people discern what is of God and what is not?

When we develop deep roots, we will "no longer be infants, tossed back and forth by the waves, and blown here and there by every wind of teaching and by the cunning and craftiness of men in their deceitful scheming. Instead, speaking the truth in love, we will in all things grow up into him who is the Head, that is, Christ" (Ephesians 4:14, 15).

#2 GROW UP

God wants us to ascend to a higher level. Healthy growth is upward in its orientation. Parents are to bring their children up, not put them down. Trees and plants grow upward toward the sun. We number grades so that students get the sense of going higher in life. We start at first grade and work toward 12th.

Justice Oliver Wendell Holmes once said, "Most people die with their music still in them." They fail to grow up, in the truest sense of the word.

Here's the answer to low self-esteem and a negative image. Christ gives us a new self-image when we follow Him. He told common, ordinary people that they were going to change the world. He told us that God cares deeply about us, and that He has even numbered the hairs on our heads, so we would understand how important we are to God.

The Cross is the measure of a person's worth. You and I were worth the death of Jesus for our sins that we might have eternal life. Christ laid down His life for us so that we would know our eternal worth. Augustine said, "People travel to wonder at the heights of the mountains, at the huge waves of the seas, at the long course of the rivers, at the vast compass of the ocean, at the circular motion of the stars—and they pass by themselves without wondering."

God wants you to *grow up*. You are endowed with talent and ability. Don't ever let anyone put you *down*. God created you to move in an upward direction, not a downward spiral. So go on to the next level. Leave the status quo and reach upward to a higher place.

#3 GROW IN

Theodore Roosevelt said, "If you are not actively becoming the person you want to be, you are becoming the person you don't want to be." We need character growth in our moods, attitudes and temperament. Who we are is more important that what we do. We focus on the substance of our lives, not the style. We talk too much about lifestyle and not enough about life-substance.

#4 GROW OUT

Grow beyond yourself. Leo Tolstoy said, "Life is a place of service." We are to live the extended life, reaching out to others in service. We grow as we serve, and as we make an investment of ourselves in others. Psychologist Alfred Adler described the highest quality of maturity as "social interest"—when the needs of others outweigh the needs of the self.

Jesus described the kingdom of God as a mustard seed.

> It is like a mustard seed, which is the smallest seed you plant in the ground. Yet when planted, it grows and becomes the largest of all garden plants, with such big branches that the birds of the air can perch in its shade (Mark 4:31, 32).

The picture of the big branches is one of our lives reaching out to provide shelter for others.

I have always been inspired by the testimony of Sadhu Singh, a Hindu who became a Christian. One day he traveled into the Himalayas to share his testimony at a monastery. Since the way was treacherous, he was guided by a monk. It was winter and they were overtaken by a fierce blizzard that came on them unexpectedly. The monk urged Sadhu to hurry, lest they freeze to death. About that time they heard the sound of a man calling for help from a deep chasm below. Sadhu insisted that they help the man. The monk refused. "If we go to help him, we will all die."

Sadhu replied, "I believe God brought me here to help this man. You go ahead. I'll stay and help him." The monk hurried on toward the monastery, while

Sadhu climbed down into the chasm to help the man, who had broken his leg. He made the best splint he could, tied the man to his back and carried him to safety. Together they limped along to the monastery. Night was falling and they could barely see the way. Suddenly they saw the lights of the monastery. Overjoyed, they started to walk faster. They stumbled and fell over an object lying in the path. It was the corpse of the monk who had left him and the injured man—frozen to death.

Their struggle was their salvation. The body heat they generated kept them alive. Later, Sadhu was asked what was the most important lesson of life he had learned. Without hesitation he said, "The most important task is to learn how to carry a burden."

#5 GROW UNIQUELY

Here is one of the most reassuring promises God gives to parents: "Train a child in the way he should go, and when he is old he will not turn from it" (Proverbs 22:6). The word *train* actually means "to nurture and guide a child according to his unique bent."

No two people are alike. We shouldn't compare ourselves with others. "We dare not classify or compare ourselves with some who commend themselves. When they measure themselves by themselves and compare themselves with themselves, they are not wise" (2 Corinthians 10:12).

God always does a unique work of grace in every person. Charles Allen tells of being a young preacher and falling into depression when he read a book about how to be a great preacher. He found liberty when he decided to be himself.

#6 GROW TOGETHER

Jesus sent His disciples out by two's to conduct their ministry. Christianity is community. Augustine said, "He cannot have God as his Father, who does not have the church as his mother."

Our relationships make us or break us. Our personalities are shaped through our interactions with others. "He who walks with the wise grows wise, but a companion of fools suffers harm" (Proverbs 13:20).

When Henry Ford was asked who was his best friend, he replied, "My best friend is the one who brings out the best in me."

Every man needs four men in his life: A Paul to mentor him, a Timothy to disciple him, a Barnabas to encourage him and a Jonathan to be a true friend.

The writer of Ecclesiastes puts the need for others in perspective:

> Two are better than one, because they have a good return for their work: If one falls down, his friend can help him up. But pity the man who falls and has no one to help him up! Also, if two lie down together, they will keep warm. But how can one keep warm alone? Though one may be overpowered, two can defend themselves. A cord of three strands is not quickly broken (Ecclesiastes 4:9-12).

#7 GROW RIGHT

Newly planted trees and plants need to be tied to a stake in the ground so they will grow straight instead of crooked. Christ is your stake. Your family is your stake. Mentors are your stake. The Bible is your stake. Tie yourself to these stakes so you will grow in the right direction.

Just as a people are trained correctly, they can also go through the wrong training. Such is the danger of unBiblical teachings and spiritual extremes. We are to "rightly divide the word of truth" (2 Timothy 2:15, *NKJV*).

In athletics and musical training, there is the need to practice right. To practice a bad habit is only to make the habit more ingrained. When we learn bad habits, we have to be trained to first unlearn them, and then be trained correctly.

Seminaries that have lost their way have ruined young ministers because they destroyed their faith. Ministers have had to unlearn the skepticism that influenced them to become men and women of faith, hope and love.

Marriages suffer because couples who grew up in dysfunctional homes act the way their parents did. They think that's how married people are supposed to act. Counseling often begins with unlearning unproductive ways of thinking and acting, before people learn news ways.

Make the most of your educational opportunities and take time to make sure the training you receive is right so that you will grow right.

#8 GROW SLOWLY

God is never in a hurry! He even took seven days to create the cosmos when He could have done so with one word. Growth takes time. We tend to want things to happen quickly. We are conditioned to the fast lane. We think God will give us an instantaneous miracle every time we hit a bump in the road. Most of the time when we pray for a miracle, we should be praying for maturity. Miracles happen quickly, maturity slowly, so we prefer miracles. Spiritual growth and personality development happen slowly over time. Small, gradual gains are made. We often take three steps forward and two steps back. But at least we're one step ahead.

Paul, the apostle, went through a long gradual development in humility, as seen in his writings. In his first letter, he introduces himself as "Paul, an apostle" (Galatians 1:1). Later, at the height of his ministry, he writes, "I am the least of the apostles" (1 Corinthians 15:9). Toward the end of his ministry, during the first Roman imprisonment, he writes, "To me, who am less than the least of all the saints" (Ephesians 3:8, *NKJV*). (A saint was the title of every believer.) Finally, in one of his last letters he admits to being the chief of sinners (see 1 Timothy 1:15).

What a downward progression, from apostle to least of the apostles, to the least of God's people, to the chief of sinners. Or was it? Was it not rather an upward ascendancy toward authentic self-awareness, freedom from pride and closeness to God?

#9 GROW STEADY

Pace yourself. Running long distances is based on finding your own pace and sticking to it. Life is not a sprint, it's a marathon. "Let us run with perseverance the race marked out for us" (Hebrews 12:1).

Running is my primary exercise. I run every day. I have to run at my own pace and not try to keep up with anyone else. I have to conserve my energy so I can complete the course I've chosen. This means exerting my will over my body and mastering my emotions.

Spiritual growth boils down to pressing on when you feel like quitting the race. "I press on to take hold of that for which Christ Jesus took hold of me" (Philippians 3:12). Great things happen little by little. Practice the spiritual disciplines of prayer, meditation of Scripture, worship, giving and service and you will continue to grow.

#10 GROW IN LOVE

Paul says of the church: "The whole body . . . grows and builds itself up in love" (Ephesians 4:16). All true spiritual growth is growth in love. We grow in a deeper understanding of God's love, and we grow in our capacity to love others even as God loves us.

Christianity is a revolution of love. The American Red Cross was gathering supplies, medicine, clothing and food for the suffering people of Biafra. Inside one of the boxes that showed up at the collecting depot one day was a letter that read: "We have recently been converted to Christ and because of our conversion, we want to try to help. We won't ever need these again. Can you use them for something worthwhile?" Inside the box was Ku Klux Klan sheets. The sheets were cut into strips and eventually used to bandage the wounds of the suffering in Africa.

When Dick Hoyt was 59, his 37-year-old son, Rick, told him he wanted to compete in a 5K race. Rick, who had cerebral palsy, was confined to a wheelchair and could only communicate by touching a computer modem with his knee and forehead. Dick pushed his son through town in his wheelchair to complete the 5K marathon. Rick told his dad he didn't feel handicapped when he crossed the finish line. Later, they decided to compete in the greatest race in North America—the Iron Man Triathlon.

Dick put his son in a raft and swam 2½ miles in the ocean. He placed him on the front of a bike and peddled him through the hills of Hawaii 112 miles. At 8:00 p.m., after the other racers had finished, he pushed Rick 26.2 miles to complete the competition. He did this as an act of love and commitment to his son because he wanted him to cross the finish line.

Our heavenly Father is committed to getting us to the finish line of life and to meeting Him in eternity. As Paul said so confidently: "Being confident of this, that he who began a good work in you will carry it on to completion until the day of Christ Jesus" (Philippians 1:6).

GREAT FAITH

The greatest power a person can exercise is the power of faith. Not faith in faith, or in humanity, or in our abilities—but faith in God. Jesus said, "Have faith in God" (Mark 11:22).

Faith is a spiritual resource connecting humanity to God, the finite with the infinite, the temporal with the eternal, the powerless to the omnipotent. *Faith* is a gift God has given every person. "God has dealt to each one a measure of faith" (Romans 12:3, *NKJV*).

We have faith! The question is what are we going to do with it? How are we to exercise faith? How can we develop faith? Faith is trust, belief and confidence in the person, power and providence of God. "Without faith it is impossible to please God, because anyone who comes to him must believe he exists and that he rewards those who earnestly seek him" (Hebrews 11:6).

Faith comes in many shapes and sizes. The Bible speaks of those who have little faith (Matthew 6:30), others with great faith (Matthew 8:10) and those who have no faith (Mark 4:40). Some are faithless (John 20:27). Some have weak faith (Romans 14:1) while Abraham had a strong faith (Romans 4:20). Stephen was full of faith (Acts 6:5). Paul speaks of a growing faith (2 Thessalonians 1:3) and a sincere faith (2 Timothy 1:5). James describes those who are rich in faith (James 2:5) and who model a perfect or mature faith (James 2:22). Finally, Peter speaks of a precious faith, which means unique and special (2 Peter 1:1).

The power of faith is seen throughout Scripture. Faith in God brings success, blessing and prosperity. "Believe in the Lord your God and so shall you be established; believe his prophets, and you shall prosper" (2 Chronicles 20:20, *NKJV*).

Jesus said that faith moves mountains and makes the impossible possible:

"I tell you the truth, if you have faith as small as a mustard seed, you can say to this mountain, 'Move from here to there' and it will move. Nothing will be impossible for you" (Matthew 17:20).

Faith is the only requirement for salvation and receiving the gift of eternal life in Jesus Christ. "For it is by grace you have been saved, through faith—and this not from yourselves, it is the gift of God—not by works, so that no one can boast" (Ephesians 2:8, 9).

True faith in God and in Christ as Lord is the governing principle of one's entire life. "We live by faith, not by sight" (2 Corinthians 5:7). "The just shall live by faith" (Romans 1:17, *NKJV*).

Finally, faith gives us an overcoming attitude against fear, worry and doubt: "This is the victory that overcomes the world, even our faith" (1 John 5:4).

A famous French gymnast came to America a number of years ago and announced that he would walk on a tightrope across Niagara Falls, and he did. Three times. Then he said, "I am going to fill a wheelbarrow with dirt and rocks and roll it across too." And he did it twice. Then he asked the crowd present. "How many of you think I can roll a person across in the wheelbarrow?"

The crowd responded enthusiastically, "Yes. We believe you can!"

The gymnast turned to one man who was especially excited in his belief and said, "All right, sir, you're first. Get in." The man left running.

Let's meet the man Jesus said had the greatest faith He had ever seen. He models for us 10 commandments of great faith.

> When Jesus had entered Capernaum, a centurion came to him, asking for help. "Lord," he said, "my servant lies at home paralyzed and in terrible suffering." Jesus said to him, "I will go and heal him." The centurion replied, "Lord, I do not deserve to have you come under my roof. But just say the word, and my servant will be healed. For I myself am a man under authority, with soldiers under me. I tell this one, 'Go,' and he goes; and that one, 'Come,' and he comes. I say to my servant, 'Do this,' and he does it." When Jesus heard this, he was astonished and said to those following him, "I tell you the truth, I have not found anyone in Israel with such great faith. I say to you that many will come from the east and the west, and will take their places at the feast with Abraham, Isaac and Jacob in the kingdom of heaven. But the subjects of the kingdom will be thrown outside, into the darkness, where there will be weeping and gnashing of

teeth." Then Jesus said to the centurion, "Go! It will be done just as you believed it would." And his servant was healed at that very hour (Matthew 8:5-13).

#1 GET THE RIGHT PICTURE OF GOD

The Roman Centurion was a man who had the right concept of God. He had 100 men under his command. The backbone of the Roman army, he disciplined the troops and kept up their morale. Yet he believed in the one true God, which is the foundation of the great commandment: "Hear, O Israel: the Lord our God . . . is one" (Deuteronomy 6:4).

Faith begins with a deep understanding that not only does God exist, but He cares about us. Jesus asked, "Are not two sparrows sold for a penny? Yet not one of them will fall to the ground apart from the will of your Father. And even the very hairs of your head are all numbered. So don't be afraid; you are worth more than many sparrows" (Matthew 10:29-31).

After a men's meeting at our church, a young father shared an amusing story with me. He said, "For a while our 2 and a-half-year-old son thought you were God. One Sunday you were out of town and a guest minister preached. Our son came with us to the service instead of the children's program. On the way home, our friends asked him if he went to the children's program. He said, 'No, I went to big church,' then added, 'but God wasn't there today.'"

The man said to me, "We had no idea what he was talking about when he said God wasn't there." The next Sunday they were driving to church and picked up our radio program in the car. The little boy recognized my voice and exclaimed, "That's God talking!"

Well, needless to say, I'm not God, but the story illustrates how we confuse God with someone else or something else. We may have God confused with a minister, the church, our parents, or some fictitious notion about God. Our faith level will never rise above the picture we have of God.

God is revealed to us in Scripture as Creator, Sustainer, Redeemer and Father. He is omnipotent, omnipresent and omniscient. He is just and true in all His ways. He is "glorious in holiness, fearful in praises, doing wonders" for His people (Exodus 15:11, *NKJV*). Above all, God is love! He loves us with an everlasting love and is constantly drawing us to Himself by His loving kindness (Jeremiah 31:1). He has made us in His image and has destined us to shared eternity with Him in heaven.

When you have the right picture of God, then you will "trust in the Lord with all your heart and lean not on your own understanding; in all your ways acknowledge him, and he will make your paths straight" (Proverbs 3:5, 6).

#2 BELIEVE THE EVIDENCE

The place is important where the miracle of the healing of the Centurion's son occurred. Jesus lived in Capernaum during His ministry. It was located near Nazareth in Northern Israel, where Jesus had grown up as a boy, and where His family lived. Peter, Andrew, James and John lived in Capernaum where they had a fishing business.

While the people of Capernaum had heard the teachings of Jesus and had witnessed His miracles, they failed to believe the evidence. Later, Christ denounced them for their lack of faith.

And you, Capernaum, will you be lifted up to the skies? No, you will go down to the depths. If the miracles that were performed in you had been performed in Sodom, it would have remained to this day. But I tell you that it will be more bearable for Sodom on the day of judgment than for you (Matthew 11:23, 24).

While many in Capernaum dismissed Jesus and found reasons to explain away His miracles, the Centurion believed the evidence of Jesus' ministry.

Faith begins by believing the evidence of God's existence and His care for us seen in the Creation. "The heavens declare the glory of God; the skies proclaim the work of His hands" (Psalm 19:1). Paul says that people are without excuse for having no faith because of the clear revelation of God in Creation. "For since the creation of the world God's invisible qualities—his eternal power and divine nature—have been clearly seen, being understood from what has been made, so that men are without excuse" (Romans 1:20).

Jesus Christ himself is the greatest evidence of God. He is "the image of the invisible God" (Colossions 1:15). There is more historical evidence that Jesus lived than there is for Julius Caesar. When we look at Jesus, we look into the face of God.

We have the evidence of the impact of Christianity that has shaped Western civilization with art, literature, music, law, justice, democracy, medicine, science and technology. The great discoveries that have produced the modern age came from nations under the influence of Christianity.

We are surrounded by evidences of God's existence through personal experience. Testimonies abound of answered prayer, the miracles of God and the power of the risen Lord. History bears out the personal testimonies of faith of those who have met the risen Lord.

Your own life is marked with the fingerprints of God as He has intervened at critical moments. God has been there for you when you needed Him, even when you were unaware of Him. But today you look back at your life and see the hand of God at work.

Kepler, the astronomer, made an intricate model of our solar system. One day a friend who was an atheist came to see him at his laboratory. He noticed the impressive model and studied carefully the intricate detail of the sun and the planets set in their rotation. Turning to Kepler he said, "This is a fantastic model with amazing detail and design. Who made it?"

Seizing the opportunity to talk to his friend about God, he replied, "Nobody made it."

"Don't be ridiculous," replied his friend. "Someone had to make it." Kepler said, "Let me ask you a question. I cannot convince you that nobody made this model of our solar system and yet you believe that the grand design from which this model is taken formed itself by evolutionary chance. Tell me, by what kind of logic do you arrive at such an incongruous conclusion?"

#3 ASK GOD FOR HELP

The first reference in Scripture to prayer is Genesis 4:26: "At that time men began to call on the name of the Lord." Ours is the secular age when men have ceased to call on God. Can science, education and technology solve all our modern problems? Unequivocally, no! We need to call on God in the time of need.

God invites us: "Call on me and I will answer you and tell you great and unsearchable things you do not know" (Jeremiah 33:3).

Listen to what Jesus tells us about how to exercise faith to see results:

> Ask and it will be given to you; seek and you will find; knock and the door will be opened to you. For everyone who asks receives; he who seeks finds; and to him who knocks, the door will be opened . . . If you, then, though you are evil, know how to give good gifts to your children, how much more will your Father in heaven give good gifts to those who ask him! (Matthew 7:7, 11).

The apostle James hits the nail on the head: "You do not have because you do not ask God" (4:2).

I once read: "If you don't bother God, everything else will bother you." *Faith* means humbling ourselves before the Lord and seeking His power because we have come to the end of ourselves. "Humble yourselves, therefore, under God's mighty hand, that he may lift you up in due time. Cast all your anxiety on him because he cares for you" (1 Peter 5:6, 7). "Let us then approach the throne of grace with confidence, so that we may receive mercy and find grace to help us in our time of need" (Hebrews 4:16).

#4 CARE DEEPLY ABOUT OTHERS

The Centurion came to Jesus on behalf of his servant, not himself. Great faith is always focused on others, not on one's self. "My servant lies at home suffering," was his petition to Christ.

The greatest faith is intercessory faith. Before we can be powerful in faith, we must first be powerful in love. The servant was at a lower socioeconomic level than the Centurion. He was suffering greatly. Yet the Centurion cared for him as though he were his son. Love is no respecter of persons. The way we treat others is deeply connected with the power of faith—"Faith working through love" (Galatians 5:6, *NKJV*).

When you get involved helping others, God gets involved helping you. "If a man shuts his ears to the cry of the poor, he too will cry out and not be answered" (Proverbs 21:13).

#5 FOCUS ON JESUS

The Centurion addressed Jesus as "Lord." This is amazing when you consider the fact that to call anyone Lord except Caesar was an act of treason. Yet, he recognized the One who had all authority and power, far greater than that of the Roman empire.

Jesus is the focal point of great faith. "Fix your thoughts on Jesus" (Hebrews 3:1). I have observed three great spiritual problems in our times that keep us from focusing our faith on Jesus Christ.

Distractions. We are often like Peter who walked on the water when Jesus called him out of the boat. But when he took his eyes off Jesus and looked at the winds and waves, he doubted and sank into the waters.

Discouragement. When we go through the fires of adversity, we feel alone and abandoned by God. We lose heart and feel as though the Lord has left us. But Christ is with us through the fire just as he appeared in the flames with Shadrach, Meshach and Abed-Nego. He is the still the fourth man in the fire!

Deception. Our generation is trying to remake Jesus into less than He is. He is the Christ, the Son of the Living God. He is the eternal, incarnate Word of God, who came in all sinlessness to offer Himself as a sacrifice of atonement for the sins of the whole world and thereby secure our eternal salvation. Yet, our age is trying to reduce Him to being merely a teacher, a miracle worker, a Buddha, an enlightened one, a moralist or a prophet. But He is "the way, the truth and the life" (John 14:6). As the Centurion discerned, Jesus is *Lord!*

#6 SUBMIT TO HIS WILL

By calling Jesus "Lord," the Centurion was not demanding that Jesus do what he asked, nor was he trying to manipulate Him. He simply trusted what Jesus would do. True faith submits to God's will without question, demand or rebellion. *Trust* means to turn the situation over to God and to be content with the outcome.

Today many "faith teachers" are not teaching faith at all, but rather futile ways of manipulating God by clever prayer secrets, making a financial offering (as though God's miracles are for sale), or repeating clichés called "good confessions." Such foolishness is not faith—it is fantasy.

Can God Almighty, Creator of heaven and earth, be manipulated by mankind? If so, He would cease to be God. The Bible is clear: "Who has known the mind of the Lord? Or who has been his counselor? Who has ever given to God, that God should repay him?" (Romans 11:34, 35). God is debtor to no man. "For from him and through him and to him are all things. To him be the glory forever! Amen (v. 36).

Walking by faith means trusting in every circumstance of life—especially in tough times. C.S. Lewis likened God's use of adversity to walking a dog. If the dog gets its leash wrapped around a pole and tries to continue running forward, he will only tighten the leash more. Both the dog and the owner are after the same end, forward motion, but the owner must restrain the dog by pulling him opposite the direction he wants to go. The master, sharing the same intention but understanding better than the dog where he really wants to go, takes an action precisely opposite to that of the dog's will. In this way, God uses adversity.

#7 COME TO GOD THROUGH GRACE NOT WORKS

The Centurion expresses what many of us feel when we ask God for help: "I do not deserve for you to come to my house." We are often plagued by those four words: "I do not deserve." We find ourselves thinking and saying, "I do not deserve" the blessings of God, that job promotion, that financial blessing, the good things of life, and on and on. We suffer from a poor self-image and low self-esteem. We confuse the worthiness of God with feelings of our worthlessness. But we are made in the image of God. Our lives are endowed with divine worth and value.

Another issue in this phrase, "I do not deserve" are those who have feelings of entitlement. They believe they do deserve certain things from God—God is obligated to do what they ask, when they ask it. They need to learn the proper meaning of the phrase, "I do not deserve" and realize that all good things in life are the blessing of His grace and not our works. The Centurion had a balanced perspective on knowing his worth in God's sight and his need to ask Jesus for help without thinking he deserved it on the basis of his position, power and status.

#8 TRUST THE WORD OF GOD

The Centurion's response was so insightful that it caught Jesus off guard. In fact, Jesus was astonished by the man's spiritual insight. How astonishing that anything could astonish the Lord. But one thing that still astounds the Lord is our faith. "Speak the word and my servant will be healed." Just one word from the lips of the Son of God would bring the miracle he sought. Oh that we had the same confidence in the Word of God.

Paul said, "Faith comes by hearing the message, and the message is heard through the word of Christ" (Romans 10:17). Today we have the Word of God in the Bible. God also speaks to us through dreams and visions and by the gift of prophecy. Someone has identified 7,847 promises of God in Scripture. Every promise is a personal word from God to us. The words of Jesus are powerful. When we believe and receive them, they release the power of God to us.

Jesus' words are . . .

- *Eternal:* "Heaven and earth will pass away, but my words will never pass away" (Matthew 24:35).

- *Authoritative:* "When Jesus had finished saying these things, the crowds were amazed at his teaching, because he taught as one who had authority, and not as their teachers of the law" (Matthew 7:28, 29).

- *Powerful:* "The people were all so amazed that they asked each other, "What is this? A new teaching—and with authority! He even gives orders to evil spirits and they obey him" (Mark 1:27).

- *Gracious:* "All spoke well of him and were amazed at the gracious words that came from his lips" (Luke 4:22).

- *Spiritual:* "The Spirit gives life; the flesh counts for nothing. The words I have spoken to you are spirit and they are life" (John 6:63).

- *Life-giving:* "Simon Peter answered him, "Lord, to whom shall we go? You have the words of eternal life" (v. 68)

- *Incomparable:* " 'No one ever spoke the way this man does,' the guards declared" (7:46).

- *Judgmental:* "There is a judge for the one who rejects me and does not accept my words; that very word which I spoke will condemn him at the last day" (12:48).

- *Divine:* "He who does not love me will not obey my teaching. These words you hear are not my own; they belong to the Father who sent me" (14:24).

Great faith rests on the unalterable truth of the word of Him who cannot lie (see Hebrews 6:18).

#9 SPEAK THE WORD

Faith is found in two places: the heart and the mouth. "If you confess with your mouth, 'Jesus is Lord,' and believe in your heart God has raised him from the dead, you will be saved" (Romans 10:9). The power of faith-filled words is unmistakable. "The tongue has the power of life and death" (Proverbs 18:21). "Out of the abundance of the heart the mouth speaks" (Matthew 12:34, *NJKV*).

We too should speak the word of God by faith. "We believe; therefore, we speak" (see 2 Corinthians 4:13). God has given us great and powerful promises in His word. He gives the promise, but "the Amen is spoken by us to the glory of God" (2 Corinthians 1:20). The word *amen* means to agree with God. We cannot go around speaking words of doubt, complaint and negativism and expect to have great faith. Jesus told us to speak to the mountain and it would move and not doubt but believe that those things which we speak will come to pass.

"I tell you the truth, if anyone *says* to this mountain, 'Go, throw yourself into the sea,' and does not doubt in his heart but believes that what he *says* will happen, it will be done for him" (Mark 11:23).

#10 EXPECT RESULTS

The Centurion came to Jesus with great expectancy, and he left with great expectancy, believing what he asked for had been accomplished. "Go," Jesus told him, "It will be done as you have believed it would." When he arrived home, he found his servant healed. He asked his attendants when his health improved and learned that it was the very hour Jesus promised him his servant would be healed.

God wants us to raise our level of expectation in His power and provision. A close friend of mine told me a story about his grandfather who was a pioneer Pentecostal preacher in South Carolina. During the Great Depression, he and his family pastored a small, struggling congregation with limited finances.

One morning the family came for breakfast, but there was nothing to serve. They had run out of everything and had no money. So, he told his wife to set the table and they all sat down. He took out a piece of paper and told the kids and his wife to write down everything they wanted to buy at the grocery store. After finishing the list, they prayed and asked God to provide everything on the list.

Suddenly, there came a knock on the door. When he went to see who was there, he found no one, but the front porch was covered with grocery bags, filled to overflowing. After placing the bags on the table, they took out all the items and found everything they had written on their lists, and more!

> *"Now to him who is able to do immeasurably*
> *more than all we ask or imagine,*
> *according to his power that is at work within*
> *us . . ."* (Ephesians 3:20).

PERFECT PEACE

A very successful businessman said to me over lunch, "All the success and wealth in the world means nothing without peace of mind."

What is peace? We tend to think of peace as the absence of something—war, poverty, or stress. The Hebrew word for peace is *shalom*, which means to be in a harmony with God and others. It means to be whole, complete and fully satisfied in life. It is a common Jewish greeting—a word of blessing. The priests pronounced the shalom on the people of God. "The Lord lift up His countenance upon you and give you peace" (Numbers 6:26, *NKJV*).

The Greek word for peace is *erience*, which means "to bind together." When Christ healed a woman who suffered from a bleeding ulcer, he said to her, "Go in peace and be freed from your suffering" (Mark 5:34). Jesus binds together God and man who have been separated by sin. He brings us together, spirit, mind and body. "May your whole spirit, soul and body be kept blameless" (1 Thessalonians 5:23).

Peace comes in many forms. There is the peace of military occupation, as we see in Iraq; the peace of a chemical substance to numb our senses and dull our pain; the peace of pleasure to help us escape the pressure; the peace of prosperity that frees us. But these are often short-lived solutions.

Isaiah gives us a promise: "You will keep him in perfect peace." Then a principle: "Whose mind is stayed on you." Finally, he gives us a prerequisite: "Because he trusts in you" (Isaiah 26:3, *NKJV*).

Real peace is a gift from God. "The Lord will give strength to his people; The Lord will bless his people with peace" (Psalm 29:11, *NKJV*). "Great peace have they who love Your law, and nothing can make them stumble" (119:165). Jesus said, "Peace I leave with you; my peace I give you . . . Do not let not your hearts be troubled and do not be afraid" (John 14:27). While sitting in prison, the apostle Paul said, "Do not be anxious for anything, but in everything, by prayer and petition . . . present your requests to God. And the peace of God, which transcends all understanding, will guard your hearts and your minds in Christ Jesus" (Philippians 4:6, 7).

We feel very insecure in our world today as a result of failing relationships, economic uncertainty and the threat of terrorism. A businessman was going to Europe for two weeks. So he drove his Rolls-Royce to a downtown New York City bank and went in and asked for a loan in the amount of $5,000. The loan officer was taken aback and requested collateral. The man handed the loan officer the keys to his Rolls. The loan officer promptly had the car driven into the bank's underground parking for safe keeping and gave him the $5,000.

Two weeks later, the man walked into the bank and asked to settle his loan and get his car back. The loan officer checked the account and told him, "That will be $5,000 plus $15.40 in interest." The man wrote out a check, thanked the loan officer, and started to leave.

"Wait, sir," the loan officer said, "While you were gone, I found out that you are a multi-millionaire. Why would you need to borrow money?" The man smiled and replied, "Where else could I securely park my Rolls-Royce in Manhattan for two weeks and pay only $15.40?"

#1 BE AT PEACE WITH GOD

Have you ever seen one of those roadside signs in the North Georgia mountains that reads: "Get right with God." We don't know we are wrong with God, but we are because of sin. When Adam and Eve sinned, they hid from God. They were filled with fear. God's reconciling grace in Eden was the only cure for their fear. When they were reconciled with God, they were at peace. The Hebrew word *shalom* has its basis on the foundation of peace as atonement. God's grace covers our sins and reconciles us to Himself.

In Judges 6:24, we read that Gideon "built an altar . . . and called it the Lord is Peace." You can't have peace without an altar, and Calvary is the altar of atonement and peace. *Atonement* means "at-one-ment." God and mankind who are estranged by sin, are reconciled at Calvary. Listen to how Paul explains the cross of Christ: "God was reconciling the world to himself in Christ, not counting men's sins against them" (2 Corinthians 5:19).

Now, here's the bottom line of inner peace:

"Therefore, having been justified (that means to be right standing with God) by faith (not by works, or religious affiliation), we have peace with God through our Lord Jesus Christ (that means through Jesus' death and resurrection)" (Romans 5:1, *NKJV* [parenthesis added]).

I was asked to go to a hospital to visit a family in our church and pray for a successful businessman who had cancer. His prognosis was bleak. He lay in the bed, telling me how he could not believe it was happening to him. Just weeks before he was out playing golf, enjoying the best of life. Now he was filled with fear. He wanted to talk about his relationship with God. I prayed with him, and he released his spiritual baggage and found peace with God. When a person has peace with God, he or she can face every circumstance of life with poise, power and victory.

#2 LIVE AT PEACE WITH OTHERS

We are to "make every effort to do what leads to peace and to mutual edification" (Romans 14:19). Now that's a challenge. "If it is possible, as far as it depends on you, live at peace with everyone" (Romans 12:18). Now there's a challenge I can live with. Paul knows that it is impossible to live at peace with some people. They don't want peace; they thrive on conflict. We all know people like that. So, he tells us to live at peace as far as it depends on us. We cannot control others, but we can control our thoughts, words and actions, and make sure we are doing everything within our power to be peacemakers.

Don't be the victim of the stress and strain of others. Their baggage doesn't have to weigh you down.

The whole world can be in conflict, but you can keep a sense of inner peace. Get rid of the clutter in your relationships.

The other day I got behind a trucker with this sign on the trailer: "Those who are at war with others are not a peace with themselves" (William Hazlitt). What an odd place to find a lesson in philosophy!

#3 BE AN AGENT OF PEACE

Jesus has sent us on a peace mission. "Blessed are the peacemakers for they shall be called sons of God" (Matthew 5:9). Don't confuse being a peacemaker with being a peace keeper. Peace keepers mind other people's business and end up causing more problems. Peace keepers get triangulated in relationships and entangled in other people's conflicts. Don't become an enabler by trying to fix other people's problems. That's like trying to break up two dogs fighting. You may get more than you bargain for.

Don't stir things up with gossip and negative words. Some people can stand in the sanctuary and sing, "It Is Well With My Soul," and spread gossip before they get past the church fellowship hall. A person who will gossip to you about someone else will gossip about you to others. If you have to ask someone if they can keep something a secret, you're talking to the wrong person.

In a Peanuts cartoon, Lucy says to Charlie Brown, "I hate everything. I hate everybody. I hate the whole world!"

Charlie Brown responds, "But I thought you had inner peace."

Lucy shouts back, "I do have inner peace, but I have outer obnoxiousness."

#4 LIVE A LIFE OF INTEGRITY

The word *peace* means wholeness, which is the definition of integrity. "But the meek will inherit the land and enjoy great peace" (Psalm 37:11). "The fruit of righteousness will be peace; the effect of righteousness will be quietness and confidence forever" (Isaiah 32:17). Righteousness and peace travel hand in hand.

When we live duplicitious lives, we get fragmented in the way we think, feel and act and we lose the power of peace. When we confess our sins to God, we find peace and forgiveness that brings peace.

When Jesus washed the disciples' feet to show them the way of service, Peter blurted out, "Not just my feet but my hands and head as well." Jesus told him, "A person who has had a bath needs only to wash his feet; his whole body is clean. And you are clean . . ." (John 13:10). While we are spiritually clean, we occasionally need areas of our lives cleansed by the grace of God.

#5 CONTROL YOUR THOUGHTS

Peace is the product of wholesome thinking. "The mind of sinful man is death, but the mind controlled by the Spirit is life and peace" (Romans 8:6). I once read: "Control your thoughts. Thoughts become words, words become actions, actions become habits, habits become character, character becomes destiny." You are what you think. Emerson said, "A man is what he thinks about all day long."

#6 TRAVEL LIGHT

The Christian life is like a race. We are to "throw off everything that hinders and the sin that so easily entangles, and let us run with perseverance the race marked out for us" (Hebrews 12:1). We need to throw off everything that hinders. Jesus said, "Be careful, or your hearts will be weighed down" (Luke 21:34).

When we go on a family vacation, I like to travel light. My wife, Barbie, used to pack up everything we owned, but over the years she has learned to travel lighter. You can move about with greater ease when you travel light. So it is with life. Get rid of the excess baggage of anger, hurt feelings, disappointment, guilt, failure, grief, missed opportunities and run with perseverance in the race before you.

#7 FORGIVE . . . FORGIVE . . . FORGIVE

We're tired of hearing about forgiveness, but it is the cornerstone of peace. God's forgiveness gives us inner peace. Our forgiveness of others sets us free to enjoy life to the fullest. We need to pray the Lord's Prayer daily: "Forgive us our debts as we also have forgiven our debtors" (Matthew 6:12).

When you hold someone in bondage by refusing to forgive them, you will eventually put yourself in your own prison of bitterness and resentment. "See to it that no one misses the grace of God, and that no bitter root grows up to cause trouble and to defile many" (Hebrews 12:15).

If you are imprisoned by resentment, open the prison door with the key of forgiveness. Bring those who have hurt you before God in prayer and declare to Him that you forgive them. Then ask God to bless them and to work in their lives and you will be free.

For two years Frank and Elizabeth Morris dedicated their lives to punishing the drunken driver, Tommy Pigage, who killed their only child. Pigage, 26, left a party on December 23, 1982, after drinking too much. He was only a mile from his home when his car strayed across the center line and hit an oncoming car driven by 18-year-old Ted Morris. Ted died shortly after. Pigage was arrested for murder after his blood-alcohol level registered three times the level the law defines as intoxicating.

Driven by hatred, the Morrises monitored his court appearances, followed him to the county jail to make sure he was serving his weekend sentence and watched his apartment to try to catch him violating his probation. "We wanted him in prison," Elizabeth said. "We wanted him dead."

The hatred and bitterness were destroying them. She said, "I needed to forgive Tommy to save myself." The Morrises were there at Pigage's preliminary hearing. They wanted to see him suffer under the full penalty of the law, but the grand jury reduced the murder charge to second-degree manslaughter. Pigage's plea of not-guilty infuriated the Morrises. His trial was repeatedly postponed. This only fueled their hatred more. Finally, Pigage changed his plea to guilty and was freed on probation.

His five-year probation was unique. The judge ordered him to watch an autopsy, to ride with an ambulance crew on emergency runs and to work as a volunteer in a hospital emergency room. He was ordered to spend one night in jail every other weekend, to stop drinking and to share his experience with high school students at lectures organized by Mothers Against Drunk Driving.

Elizabeth, a group leader, was there for his first speech at a high school. She just wanted to hear what he had to say. While she expected him to say that the accident wasn't his fault, he did just the opposite. He began by referring to himself as a murderer, that he received a light sentence and that he should be in prison. He accepted full responsibility for what he did. For a moment she felt sorry for him, but back stage her compassion quickly dissipated when she smelled alcohol on his breath.

Shortly after, he violated his probation by drinking and was ordered to begin serving a 10-year jail sentence. Being Christians, the Morrises knew they had to forgive him. So Elizabeth visited him in jail to say she wanted to help him stop drinking. She continued to visit him in jail. Finally, they petitioned the judge to release him into their custody for church and other family outings. Returning from a MADD meeting, Frank stopped by the church where he served as choir director and baptized Tommy. After three months in prison, Tommy was again released on probation because of the intercession of the Morrises.[1]

#8 PRACTICE OBEDIENCE

Sometimes an ancient message is the most contemporary message we can hear. "I am the Lord your God, who teaches you what is best for you, who directs you in the way you should go. If only you had paid attention to my commands, your peace would have been like a river, your righteousness like the waves of the sea" (Isaiah 48:17, 18). *Obedience* means to act on God's Word. Remember, "faith by itself, if not accompanied by action, is dead" (James 2:17).

Obedience is simply trusting and acting on the surest counsel you will ever receive—the counsel of God in Scripture. We go to counselors to get advice and wisdom: friends, professional counselors, doctors, dentists, financial advisors, ministers, and on and on. God is the wonderful counselor and His Word is true. To fail to act on wise counsel is foolish. Most of the social, moral and economic problems of our day are the direct result of disobedience to God. God's way works best! If we trust the word of men, how much more should we trust the Word of God?

#9 CAST YOUR CARES

Paul said: "Be anxious for nothing . . . and the peace of God . . . will guard your hearts" (Philippians 4:6, 7, *NKJV*). The Greek word for *keep* is used and means placing a lid on a boiling pot. God's peace puts a lid over our hearts keeping fear out.

Anxiety is a feeling of blind apprehensive fear; a general sense of foreboding. Anxiety haunts us with the question "What if?"

- What if I get sick?

- What if my marriage fails?

- What if my teenager rebels?

- What if I lose my job?

- What if my stock portfolio loses value?

- What if I don't have enough for retirement?

- What if I get a serious illness?

Peter said, "Cast all your anxiety on him because he cares for you" (1 Peter 5:7).

The answer to the anxious *what if?* is a triumphant *I know!*

- *I know God loves and cares for me.*

- *I know God will never leave me nor forsake me.*

- *I know nothing can separate me from God's love.*

- *I know that no weapon formed against me will prosper. I know that God is for me, with me and in me.*

- *I know that not one word of all God's promises have failed.*

- *I know I am more than a conqueror.*

Mark Twain said, "I've suffered through a great many catastrophes in life; most of which have never happened." Anxiety is considered to be the basis of all psychological problems. Panic attacks, or anxiety attacks, can render us emotionally paralyzed. At least one in four Americans, about 65 million, will experience an anxiety disorder at some point in their lifetime.[2]

Jesus walks by and says to us: "Do not worry about your life, what you will eat or drink; or about your body, what you will wear. . . . your heavenly Father knows that you need them. But seek first his kingdom and his righteousness, and all these things will be given to you as well. Therefore do not worry about tomorrow, for tomorrow will worry about itself. Each day has enough trouble of its own (Matthew 6:25, 32-34).

#10 EXPERIENCE HIS PRESENCE

While running for his life, David penned these words: "In your presence is fullness of joy" (Psalm 16:11, *NKJV*). God says: "Be still and know that I am God" (Psalm 46:10). We have to be still in God's presence to find peace. Until we are still, we will know neither God's person nor his power.

David said, "My soul finds rest in God alone" (Psalm 62:1). Personal times of worship, reading Scripture and reflection usher us into the presence of the Lord. "We set our hearts at rest in his presence" (1 John 3:19). By the presence of the Lord, I don't mean its omnipresence. That's a given. But people go through life unaware of His presence, even though God is all around them. By the presence of the Lord, I mean His experienced presence. As Peter said, "Times of refreshing shall come from the presence of the Lord" (Acts 3:19, KJV). God meets us in the place of quiet reflection and prayer, speaks to us in His still, small voice, and fills our hearts with perfect peace.

This paraphrase of Psalm 23 by Tokio Megashio says it best:

> *The Lord is my pace setter, I shall not rush.*
> *He makes me stop and rest for quiet intervals,*
> *He provides me with images of stillness which deepen*
>   *my serenity.*

*He leads me in ways of efficiency through calmness of
    mind,*
And His guidance is peace.
*Even though I have a great many things to accom-
    plish each day,*
I will not fret, for His presence is here.
*His timelessness, His all importance will keep me in
    balance.*
*He prepares refreshment and renewal in the midst of
    my activity.*
By anointing my mind with oils of tranquillity
My cup of joyous energy overflows.
*Surely harmony and effectiveness shall be the fruits of
    my hours.*
For I shall walk in the pace of the Lord,
And dwell in His house forever.

Endnotes

[1] "Frank and Elizabeth Morris Forgive Tommy Pigage," *New York Times*, 22 Aug. 1988.

[2] Edward M. Hallowell, "Why Worry?" *Psychology Today*, Nov./Dec. 1997: 36.

SPIRITUAL
WISDOM

John D. Rockefeller got into a taxi cab one day as he
departed the airport en route to a business meeting. The cab driver recognized him and said, "Mr.
Rockefeller, I have some money and I want to invest it.
What should I do?"

Rockefeller replied, "Make wise decisions."

"Well, that sounds great, but tell me, how do I make
wise decisions?"

Rockefeller said, "Experience."

"Yes, but how do I get experience?" the cabby asked.

Rockefeller said, "Make bad decisions."

Wisdom is the key to success in any endeavor.
"Wisdom is supreme, therefore get wisdom. Though it
cost all you have, get understanding" (Proverbs 4:7).
Wisdom must become our top priority if we expect to
be successful.

The Hebrew word for wisdom is *chokmah,* which
means "the skill for godly living and the ability to live
life in a God-honoring way." While knowledge is infor-
mation, wisdom is insight; the ability to apply knowledge in a given set of circumstances.

Worldly wisdom can be destructive: "There is a way
that seems right to a man but in the end it leads to

death" (Proverbs 16:25). The apostle Paul asks, "Where is the wise man? Where is the scholar? Where is the philosopher of this age? Has not God made foolish the wisdom of the world? . . . For the foolishness of God is wiser than man's wisdom" (1 Corinthians 1:20, 25).

Spiritual wisdom comes from God and leads to life. David prayed, "You teach me wisdom in the inmost place" (Psalm 51:6). "Blessed is the man who finds wisdom, the man who gains understanding" (Proverbs 3:13). "Wisdom makes one wise man more powerful than ten rulers in a city" (Ecclesiastes 7:19). The prophet Daniel said, "Those who are wise will shine like the brightness of the heavens" (Daniel 12:3).

Jesus himself "grew in wisdom and stature, in favor with God and men" (Luke 2:52). Obviously, there is wisdom that is higher than the wisdom of man that comes to us from God. The early church looked for leaders who were "full with the Spirit and wisdom" (Acts 6:3). There is earthly wisdom and heavenly wisdom. "But the wisdom that comes from heaven is first of all pure" (James 3:17).

Does not wisdom call out? Does not understanding raise her voice?

On the heights along the way, where the paths meet, she takes her stand; beside the gates into the city, at the entrances she cries aloud:

> To you, O men, I call out; I raise my voice to all mankind. Choose my instruction instead of silver, knowledge rather than choice gold, for wisdom is more precious than rubies, and nothing you desire can compare with her (Proverbs 8:1-4, 10, 11).

Here's a humorous look at our need for wisdom. A small commuter airplane was approaching an airport.

Pilot to control tower: "What time is it?"

Control tower to pilot: "What airline is this?"

Pilot to control tower: "What difference does that make?"

Control tower to pilot: "If this is British Airways, it is 1800 hours; if it is American Airlines, it's 6 p.m.; if this is a commuter airline, the big hand is on the . . ."

When I grew up, we had family devotions. My father typically read passages from the books of Proverbs, James or First Peter. Proverbs was his favorite. When I asked him why he always read from Proverbs he said, "Because it is filled with common sense and you kids need it." Well, common sense is not so common anymore.

Let's take a walk through the Book of Proverbs and discover the keys to obtaining spiritual wisdom.

#1 PURSUE WISDOM AS YOUR TOP PRIORITY

Solomon said, "Wisdom is supreme." Why? When we get wisdom, we get everything that comes with it. Wisdom is a package deal, with a lot of perks and benefits. Wisdom brings wealth, honor and long life. Wisdom "is a tree of life to those who embrace her; those who lay hold of her will be blessed" (Proverbs 3:18).

When Solomon became king, God appeared to him in a dream and said, "Ask for whatever you want me to give you" (1 Kings 3:5). I wonder how we would respond to such an invitation by God. Solomon answered, "Give your servant a discerning heart to govern your people and to distinguish between right and wrong" (v. 9). The Lord was pleased with his request and said, "I will do what you have asked . . . Moreover, I will give you what you have not asked for—both riches and honor—so that in your lifetime you will have no equal among kings" (vv. 12, 13).

Wisdom brings safety. "Wisdom will save you from the ways of wicked men" (Proverbs 2:12). During the days of intense persecution in Scotland, a young Christian girl was stopped by the police while on her way to attend a secret Christian meeting. "Where are you going," they asked. Terrified, yet not wanting to lie she whispered a prayer, "Lord, give me wisdom." Then she said, "My elder brother has died, and I'm going to hear His will read, to receive my part in the inheritance." That's wisdom.

#2 FEAR THE LORD

Here's where wisdom starts: "The fear of the Lord is the beginning of knowledge" and "the beginning of wisdom" (Proverbs 1:7; 9:10). Now here's a concept you don't hear much about any more—the fear of the Lord. The fear the Lord is to reverence Him and to give Him the rightful place of authority by honoring and obeying Him. "To fear of the Lord teaches a man wisdom, and humility comes before honor" (15:33).

Gibbons in *The Decline and Fall of the Roman Empire,* cites five major factors in the demise of Rome: Undermining of the dignity and sanctity of the home; escalating taxes to fund welfare programs and circuses for the people; the mad craze for pleasure; building of great military armaments while neglecting the real enemy within—moral decay; and the decay of religion. There was no fear of God in Rome.

Listen to this promise: God "will be the sure foundation for your times, a rich store of salvation and wisdom and knowledge; the fear of the Lord is the key to this treasure" (Isaiah 33:6).

#3 STAY OFF THE PATH OF THE UNRIGHTEOUS

The first Bible verse I taught my son was Proverbs 1:10: "My son, when sinners entice you do not give in to them." I have taught it to my daughter as well. Temptation comes most often from peer pressure. Peer pressure doesn't stop after adolescence.

Wisdom means standing up for what you believe and being true to your convictions regardless of peer pressure. "Blessed is the man who does not walk in the counsel of the wicked or stand in the way of sinners or sit in the seat of mockers" (Psalm 1:1). We are to avoid . . .

1. *The belief system of the world.* "Do not walk in the counsel of the ungodly." The word *counsel* means "schemes, advice, plans and patterns." The word *ungodly* (*rasha,* Hebrew) means "to be out of joint;" to be out of step with God.

2. *The behavior of the world.* "Do not stand in the way of sinners." The word for *sinners* (*chatta,* Hebrew) means "to miss the mark." It is a mistaking of the way and speaks of habitual sinning with no desire to change.

3. *The belonging of the world.* "Do not sit in the seat of the mockers." The word for *mockers* (*lesim,* Hebrew) means "a cynical and arrogant contempt for God; scornful." It describes the self-sufficient person who boasts of his complete independence from God.

Someone asked the great preacher Dwight L. Moody if he would have to give up the world when he became a Christian. Moody replied, "No. The world will give you up."

The way of wisdom is the way of the moral high ground. *Righteousness* is that which is in conformity to the will of God. The unrighteous cut corners. For them, the end justifies the means. But God sees what we do, and He will judge us accordingly.

We often stand at the crossroads in decisions and face the two roads Jesus described: The broad road that leads to destruction and the narrow road that leads to life. *Wisdom* means choosing wisely the narrow road, or what Robert Frost called "the road less traveled."

#4 GUARD YOUR HEART

"Guard your heart for it is the wellspring of life" (Proverbs 4:23). The heart is the core of our being—our thoughts, feelings, attitudes, values and philosophy of life. Jesus said, "Out of the overflow of the heart the mouth speaks" (Matthew 12:34).

We are to guard what enters our minds. The mind is continually bombarded with sights, sounds and images marketing the philosophy of this present age. The United Negro College Fund has used a fantastic motto for many years: "The mind is a terrible thing to waste."

You also need to guard the deposit of truth that has been placed in your heart. If you were fortunate enough to have been raised in a Christian home and loving church, treasure the wealth of truth that has been deposited in the safety deposit box of your heart. The greatest inheritance parents can leave their children is not a financial inheritance but a faith inheritance. "Guard the good deposit that was entrusted to you—guard it with the help of the Holy Spirit" (2 Timothy 1:14).

There are some people who will try to steal a person's faith because they are so unsure of their own beliefs. It reminds me of the freshman college professor who ridiculed the miracles in the Bible to the class. He took special issue with the story of Jonah and the whale.

One student who was offended spoke up in defense of her faith. "I believe all the miracles of the Bible are true."

"You even believe that Jonah was swallowed by a whale?" he asked in disbelief.

"Yes I do," she replied, "and when I get to heaven, I plan to ask him what it was like to be inside the belly of a whale for three days."

Thinking he would outwit her, he snapped back, "Suppose he's not in heaven for you to ask."

She replied, "Well, then, you ask him."

The movie *The Passion of the Christ* by Mel Gibson has the whole world in a buzz. Controversy and praise surrounds the film. Personally, I believe the film is a wake-up call by God to draw our attention back to the centerpiece of history—the Cross where Jesus made atonement for our sins and secured for us eternal life. The Cross is the highest display of the wisdom of God in human history. "The message of the cross is foolishness to those who are perishing, but to us who are being saved it is the power of God" (1 Corinthians 1:18).

I don't want to preach to the choir, so let me say to you if you are not a Christian, ponder the Cross and ask God to show you what Jesus accomplished on the

Cross for you. Jesus died for *your* sins. The Cross is a personal matter. He rose again on the third day for *your* justification—that means to be made righteous before God. Here's God's promise: "If you confess with your mouth, 'Jesus is Lord,' and believe in your heart God raised him from the dead you will be saved" (Romans 10:9).

#5 SUBMIT TO GOD'S DISCIPLINE

Let's be honest: We all like to avoid pain and gain pleasure, but we will have to submit to the Lord's discipline if we want to be wise.

I sat in counseling with a young woman who was going through a very difficult personal situation. She had been abused and neglected by a man she was dating. She asked me why he had treated her the way he did. What could explain such harsh behavior?

I explained to her that the sin nature seeks to do two things: minimize pain and maximize pleasure. In his mind, she had become a barrier to his personal happiness. He treated her that way because he wanted to experience pleasure and didn't want anything causing him discomfort. As soon as their relationship required certain commitments from him, he turned against her and left her.

Spiritual discipline helps us to grow out of the immature pattern of endlessly trying to obtain pleasure and avoiding pain. Listen to this invaluable counsel:

> My son, do not make light of the Lord's discipline, and do not lose heart when he rebukes you . . . we have all had human fathers who disciplined us and we respected them for it. How much more should we submit to the Father of

our spirits and live! . . . God disciplines us for our good, that we may share in his holiness. No discipline seems pleasant at the time, but painful. Later on, however, it produces a harvest of righteousness and peace for those who have been trained by it (Hebrews 12:5-11).

#6 HOLD YOUR TONGUE AND AVOID PEOPLE WHO TALK TOO MUCH

I once read, "Better to be thought a fool than to open one's mouth and remove all doubt." The more we talk, the less we say. "When words are many, sin is not absent" (Proverbs 10:19).

Novelist George Eliot said, "Blessed is the man who having nothing to say abstains from giving us wordy evidence of the fact." Proverbs 21:23 says, "He who guards his mouth and his tongue keeps himself from calamity."

If you have to ask others whether or not they can keep something you tell them a secret, then the answer is obvious and the question, rhetorical. People who talk to you negatively about others, will talk about you in the same manner.

Let's be real with each other. We all say things we wish we never said. We wish we could take back many of the things we say in haste, or in a moment of anger or impulsivity. Once we say something, we can never take back the words. Let's make a conscious effort to guard our words more carefully.

A couple from Brooklyn went to a high society party of intellectuals. The conversation came up about Mozart. "Absolutely brilliant!" Remarked one man. "What a prodigy!" Said a woman.

Anxious to join the conversation the woman from Brooklyn blurted out, "Ah, Mozart! Only this morning I saw him get on the No. 5 bus to Coney Island!" There was a sudden hush. Her husband was mortified. He pulled her aside.

"Get your coat," he whispered. "We're leaving." And he hustled her out the door.

"What's wrong?" She asked. "Are you angry about something?"

"I've never been so embarrassed in my life!" He replied. "You saw Mozart take the No. 5 bus to Coney Island. You idiot! Don't you know the No. 5 bus doesn't go to Coney Island?"

#7 WALK WITH THE WISE

"He who walks with the wise grows wise, but a companion of fools suffers harm" (Proverbs 13:20). Look at the proof of a person's life before you allow him/her to influence you. Don't be fooled by superficial success. Get to know the real person.

Jackie Robinson made history in 1947 by becoming the first black major league baseball player for the Brooklyn Dodgers. Branch Rickey, the owner of the Dodgers, told Robinson that it would be tough for him in the league, but that he would support him all the way. Jackie endured abuse and racial slurs—especially in the beginning of his career. One particular game, Robinson missed two ground balls at second base. The crowd booed him without mercy. Then, suddenly right in the middle of the game, his teammate Pee Wee Reese, the immortal Dodgers shortstop, walked over and put his arm around Jackie. Jackie Robinson later said. "That may have saved my career. Pee Wee made me feel like I belonged."

#8 KEEP YOURSELF HUMBLE

It's hard for us to get a grip on humility. We all know we need it, but if we admit we have it, we have proven that we lack it. What a catch 22! Humility is dependency on God—service toward others and an honest appraisal of self. That's all.

A college professor wrote a remark at the end of one of my papers that continues to make an impact on me. The paper addressed an issue I had debated the teacher about in class. The paper proved my case, which he admitted he had been wrong on that point. But his remarks "got my goat": *David, you have an equal talent for research and for writing. Keep yourself humble and you will go far.*

I won the battle; he won the war. We have to stay humble and avoid the pitfall of pride. "Pride goes before destruction and a haughty spirit before a fall" (Proverbs 16:18). Here is a great promise and a solemn caution: "God resists the proud but gives grace to the humble" (James 4:6, *NKJV*).

#9 LISTEN TO ADVICE

No one develops wisdom in a vacuum. We need other people to pour their knowledge, discernment and experience into our lives. "Listen to advice and accept instruction, and in the end you will be wise" (Proverbs 19:20).

We gain advice from parents, counselors, colleagues, friends and mentors. "As iron sharpens iron, so one man sharpens another" (Proverbs 27:17). We need relationships with iron enough to sharpen our judgment and our character. True friends will tell us the truth. "The wounds of a friend can be trusted, but an enemy multiplies kisses" (v. 6).

It's one thing to get wisdom and another to follow it. Jesus said, "Don't throw your pearls to pigs" (Matthew 7:6). That means don't tell anyone something they are not ready to hear. If you do, Jesus said, they will tear you to pieces. People get angry about unwanted advice.

Solomon's son, Rehoboam, lost the kingdom because he shunned the advice of the elders. He sought their advice, but when he got it, he intentionally acted on the foolish counsel he received from his peers (see 2 Chronicles 10). The kingdom of Judah fell to the Babylonian army and went into exile because King Zedekiah refused Jeremiah's counsel, even after he had a private meeting to receive counsel (see Jeremiah 34:14-28).

The Hebrew word translated *hear* in the Old Testament actually means "to obey." If we truly seek wise counsel, we should act on it.

#10 ASK GOD FOR WISDOM

Wisdom is in proportion to our communion with God. Solomon's great wisdom came as a result of prayer. No one can counsel you like the Wonderful Counselor! Human counsel is good, but nothing can compare with hearing from God in prayer. God invites us: "Call on me, and I will answer you and show you great and mighty things you do not know" (Jeremiah 33:3).

Here is a magnificent promise: "If any one lacks wisdom, he should ask God, who gives generously to all without finding fault, and it will be given to him" (James 1:5). Prayer sharpens the mind, clears our thinking and gives us access to the creativity of God.

The eminent industrialist Robert G. LeTourneau, manufacturer of earth-moving equipment, received a wartime order from the government to develop a machine that would lift airplanes. No such machine had ever been conceived, much less built. LeTourneau and his engineers went to work on the problem. They were baffled. Every think-tank session came up empty. Frustration set in.

One Wednesday, as evening approached, the team was feverishly at work. LeTourneau got up from the meeting and said, "Well, fellows, I'm leaving to go to prayer meeting at my church."

"Prayer meeting?" they said. "You can't do that. We've got a deadline to meet."

"But I've got a deadline with God," he replied emphatically. He went on to the prayer meeting. Forgetting his problem, he entered into singing with the congregation and praying with others about their needs. On his way home, while walking down the street, he reported that suddenly, the complete design of the machine appeared in his mind—complete with every detail.

I ran across a new definition of prayer that said: "Prayer is bringing the whole of life into the light of God's presence for cleansing and decision."

True
Success

Two cows were grazing in a pasture when they saw a milk truck pass by. On the side of the truck were the words, "Pasteurized, homogenized, standardized, vitamin A added." One cow sighed and said to the other, "Makes you feel sort of inadequate, doesn't it?"

I'm sure that's how Joshua must have felt when God called him to follow Moses.

- Moses the man of God.

- Moses who withstood Pharaoh and brought Egypt to its knees.

- Moses who parted the Red Sea.

- Moses who brought Manna from Heaven.

- Moses who brought water from the rock.

- Moses who received the law of God in stone.

- Moses who spoke with God face to face.

- Moses who saw the glory of God.

- Moses who led Israel through the wilderness for 40 years.

His name is still revered to this day. One can only imagine the enormity of this man's influence at the height of his ministry. Moses, however, would not lead Israel into the Promised Land. This would be the responsibility of Joshua, Moses' personal aide and close friend, who had accompanied Moses throughout the wilderness. Joshua needed a success strategy, and so do we. *Success* simply means reaching your desired goals. It is accomplishing what you set out to accomplish. Success also means to be prosperous and victorious.

> After the death of Moses the servant of the Lord, the Lord said to Joshua son of Nun, Moses' aide: "Moses my servant is dead. Now then, you and all these people, get ready to cross the Jordan River into the land. . . . I will give you every place where you set your foot, as I promised Moses. Your territory will extend from the desert to Lebanon, and from the great river, the Euphrates—all the Hittite country—to the Great Sea on the west. No one will be able to stand up against you all the days of your life. As I was with Moses, so I will be with you; I will never leave you nor forsake you.
>
> Be strong and courageous, because you will lead these people to inherit the land I swore to their forefathers to give them. Be strong and very courageous. Be careful to obey all the law my ser-vant Moses gave you; do not turn from it to the right or to the left, that you may be successful wherever you go. Do not let this Book of the Law depart from your mouth; meditate on it day and night, so that you may be careful to do everything

written in it. Then you will be prosperous and successful. Have I not commanded you? Be strong and courageous. Do not be terrified; do not be discouraged, for the Lord your God will be with you wherever you go (Joshua 1:1-9).

Here are the 10 steps of true success we learn from God's promises to Joshua.

#1 ATTITUDE

Attitude is one's mental outlook on life. Some say attitude is everything. It's not, but it is a big part of the equation of success. God told Joshua to meditate and to speak the word of God (at that time the writings of Moses). Why? Because the Word of God shapes the way we think and gives us a spiritual mind. "For as he thinks in his heart, so is he" (Proverbs 23:7, *NKJV*).

We need a spiritual mind to be truly successful. The worldly system that defines success only in terms of fame, fortune, power and pleasure, falls short in providing true success. The Word of God outlines a plan for a truly successful life that brings glory to God. "To be carnally minded is death, but to be spiritually minded is life and peace" (Romans 8:6, *NKJV*).

God calls us to a positive attitude of faith. "Be strong and courageous!" We need to cultivate an attitude of success before we can achieve it. Success starts in the mind.

God created us to succeed. At the dawn of Creation, God pronounced His blessing on us: "God blessed them and said, 'Be fruitful and increase in number; fill the earth and subdue it'" (Genesis 1:28). I call this the Genesis Commission. God wants each of us to be fruitful, to increase, to fill and to subdue.

"In everything [David] did he had great success, because the Lord was with him" (1 Samuel 18:14). The same God is with us to give us success.

The psalmist tells us that we are crowned with glory and honor and that we have been given dominion over all the works of God's hands (Psalm 8:4-8). Jesus says, "Come, follow me, and I will make your fishers of men" (Matthew 4:19). Jesus empowers us to make an eternal impact for the kingdom of God and that is the bottom line of true success.

We can have the successful attitude of Paul who declared, "I can do all things through Christ who strengthens me" (Philippians 4:13, *NKJV*). Finally, the apostle John says, "Beloved, I pray that you may prosper in all things and be in health just as your soul prospers" (3 John 2, *NKJV*).

Avoid the negatives. We need to guard our hearts and minds against three negative attitudes that keep us from success: cowardice, complaint and criticism. If you stop and think about it, these three attitudes kept Israel from possessing the Promised Land during the days of Moses and kept them wandering the desert for 40 years. And these attitudes will keep us in the desert. Israel was afraid of the giants in the land, complained about life in the desert and criticized Moses, God's appointed leader.

Accentuate the positives. The spiritual mind is guided by three attitudes. Faith that dares to believe God for great and mighty things, hope that always looks on the bright side of things, and love that honors God and seeks the best for others.

It's like the man who decided to become a monk. He joined a monastery and took a vow of silence for three years. He was only allowed to speak two words at the end of a year. After the first year, he went to the head of the monastery and said, "Hard bed."

After the second year, "Cold food."

After the third year, "I quit."

"Good," replied the master, "you haven't done anything but complain since you got here!"

#2 ACCOUNTABILITY

Joshua was called of God and he answered that call: "The Lord said to Joshua" (1:1). Your vocation is your calling. Your career is your place of ministry. You don't have to go looking for a ministry. Your ministry is where you live and work and play.

I want to ask you something. Are you doing what you're doing in life because God has called you to do it? If not, then why are you doing it? And if you can say that God has called you into that career, are you treating it like a calling—more than just a job or a position?

The calling of God requires you to be responsible and accountable to God for your life. Your life is God's gift to you, what you do with your life is your gift to God. "So then, each of us will give an account of himself to God" (Romans 14:12).

"Yes, but" is the confession of every failure. Winners take responsibility and don't make excuses or blame others. Passing the buck is the great America pastime. People will never succeed until they take charge of their lives and stop making excuses and blaming others.

Success must be handled with accountability to God. When God gives us a place of influence, we are to handle it with care. When I was a boy, my friend and

I were out riding our bikes when we came upon an electrical power plant. We thought about climbing up on some of the structures and exploring, but we could hear the loud sound of the buzz coming through the wires. We knew the power of electricity. We decided, wisely I might add, to stay off everything in that plant. Anyone who aspires for greatness should understand the cost of power and responsibility that comes with it.

#3 APTITUDE

God told Joshua, "Get ready to cross the Jordan river" (Joshua 1:2). Joshua was prepared for his ministry because of the training he had with Moses. Paul told Timothy to "Do your best to present yourself to God as one approved, a workman who does not need to be ashamed and who correctly handles the word of truth" (2 Timothy 2:15). We have to get ready for success. Opportunity knocks on the door of preparation.

We maximize our aptitude, first, by developing our talents, gifts and abilities. Keep on growing. We need ongoing training, education and preparation of our skills and gifts. No one has arrived at perfection or full efficiency. We all have room to grow and to learn. Without developing our aptitude, we never achieve our potential. Talent and abilities alone will never bring success until they are developed to their maximum efficiency.

I have been a musician since I was 8. But musical ability means nothing without arduous training and constant practicing. Athletic aptitude must be submitted to training and discipline for athletes to reach their potential. Success requires continual learning and training, or else we grow stagnant and out of touch with our career field.

Some great business men of yesterday haven't been in active business management and leadership for years, yet they try to consult younger business men and women. But the business world is changing rapidly. Being an expert is not a permanent status. Yesterday's solutions won't always solve today's problems.

You also need to discern your strengths and your weaknesses. Play to your strengths and avoid your weaknesses. Surround yourself with a team of qualified leaders and workers who make up for your aptitude deficiencies so you can do what you do best.

Use what God has given you. You have to move from preparing for work and get started doing something. You have to move on from pre-season training and get in the game. "Each one should use whatever gift he has received to serve others, faithfully administering God's grace in its various forms" (1 Peter 4:10).

You have infinite God-given potential. You don't need more gifts, abilities or opportunities. You just need to use what God has given you. "His divine power has given us everything we need for life and godliness" (2 Peter 1:3).

I want to ask you a question: *What's in your hand?* What gifts, talents, abilities and opportunities has God given you that you can use for His glory?

At the burning bush, when Moses offered God one excuse after the other as to why he was inadequate to lead the Israelites out of Egypt, God asked him, "What's in your hand?" Moses replied, "A staff." Yet God anointed the shepherd's staff that brought Egypt to its knees, parted the Red Sea and secured water from a rock in the wilderness.

David, "What's in your hand?" "Just a slingshot and five smooth stones." But God used it to defeat Goliath and to reignite the confidence of the army of Israel.

Elijah, the prophet, "What's in your hand?" "Just a handful of flour and a cup of oil." Yet, he prayed over it in faith, and God multiplied it, providing an endless supply for a single mother and her son during a time of famine.

"Little boy, what's in your hand?" "Just five loaves and two fish." But when he put them in the hands of Jesus, the Lord fed a multitude.

Paul, the apostle, "What's in your hand while you sit in prison?" "Just a pen and parchment." But he wrote two-thirds of the New Testament.

Martin Luther, "What's in your hand?" "Just the Book of Romans." But when he read it, he discovered that "The just shall live by faith." He wrote the 95 Theses, tacked them on the front door of the Wittenburg Church and started a spiritual reformation in Germany.

"Handel, what's in your hand?" "Just a musical gift." Yet, in a time of deep depression, he composed *The Messiah* and inspired the world.

Billy Graham, "What's in your hand?" "Just radio and TV airwaves." He used them to preach the gospel of Christ to hundreds of millions around the world.

Mother Theresa, "What's in your hand?" "Just a heart of compassion." But she went to India at the call of God to care for "the least of these" and showed the world the depth of God's love.

Martin Luther King Jr. "What's in your hand?" "Just a single voice." Yet, he proclaimed liberty to those captive in segregation and discrimination and issued forth the Civil Rights Movement.

You don't need anything more to succeed. Just dedicate your resources to God, put them to use and God will bless your efforts with great success.

#4 ASPIRATION

God's words to Joshua, "get ready to cross the Jordan River into the land I am about to give to them" (Joshua 1:1), increased Joshua's desire to accomplish something great for God with his life by conquering and settling the Land of Promise. The emphasis for Joshua was on *the land*. Joshua had sought to claim the Promised Land 40 years earlier when he and 11 others were sent by Moses to spy out the land. He and Caleb wanted to possess it, but because of fear and unbelief the other 10 spies caused the whole nation to miss their opportunity.

Now here is what is amazing—Joshua's desire to possess the land was not diminished by having to wander 40 years in the wilderness because of the disobedience of others. He still aspired to do the will of God.

Don't let anyone or anything diminish your desires or put out the fire of your passion.

All success begins with desire— a burning passion to accomplish something great. Desire gives rise to a vision and then to a plan of action. Spiritual leadership begins with such desire: "If anyone sets his heart on being an overseer he desires a noble task," says the apostle Paul (1 Timothy 3:1). Success starts with "setting your heart" on something you want to accomplish.

We need to take initiative in reaching our goals. Initiative is self-motivated creativity—the ability to do what needs to be done without being asked or told to do it. Too many people today are waiting for life to happen to them. You have to go out there and make a place for yourself in the world. You have to go and make it happen!

During college, I had a summer job in underground Atlanta working on a construction crew. We were laying underground pipe for the Marta mass transit system. My first day, I was given the job of being a flag man. I was handed an orange flag and told to direct traffic around our job site. All day long I stood in the hot sun. It was the longest day of my life, and I have never been more bored than I was that day.

I told myself I had to get a better position than that or I would die from boredom. So the next day, I started looking the crew over for guys who acted like they wanted to get out of work. Two guys were working on the ditch that was being prepared for the pipelines. One guy complained off and on for a couple of hours about being in the ditch.

Finally, I said to him, "Hey, do you want a break from that ditch? You can wave this flag for a while and I'll take your place." He was thrilled to get out of the ditch and I was thrilled to get in it. I am into upward mobility, and sometimes the way up is the way down.

I made myself available for every type of work I could get on that summer job. The foreman noticed my initiative and gave me a number of opportunities to learn new tasks. I learned to build the underground metal tunnels and laid the pipe myself for Southern Bell and Georgia Power. After that first day, I never waved that flag again.

If you show initiative, someone will take notice and you will be promoted. Initiative is the secret to upward mobility.

#5 ADMINISTRATION

Let's draw another lesson from God's charge to "Get ready." Getting ready to accomplish a goal means to attend to administrative details. Later, Joshua tells the officers of the people, "Get your supplies ready." Great projects require detailed administrative work. Success is not all lights and glamour. Somebody's got to mind the store.

The word *administration* comes from a Greek nautical term that means "to navigate a ship through storms and treacherous waters into safe port." Joshua would face challenges with people and situations he could not anticipate. All great endeavors have unforeseen challenges. The question is: Can we navigate our way through them?

Plan your work. The Book of Joshua contains battle strategies that were used during the Six-Day War of 1967. Can you imagine modern-day generals consulting the Book of Joshua? They did. Why? Because Joshua never lost a battle.

You always want to follow in the steps of a successful person. His military and political successes are a testimony to his high level of administrative preparation.

Work your plan. Once you get your plan together, implement it until you finish. Don't get off focus. Don't overreact to every demand, interruption and emergency.

I've worked with people who started off with a great plan, then forgot all about it. They ended up drifting aimlessly in their work because they forget what it was they set out to do. I call it APD—attention plan disorder. When Mother Teresa was once asked why people loose their spiritual passion, she replied, "Distractions."

#6 ACTION

God gave Joshua a great promise: "I will give you every place you set your foot" (Joshua 1:3). But if you don't set your foot, you won't get anywhere. God honors action. Promises have to be possessed! There comes the time to move from preparation to performance.

Thomas J. Peters and Robert H. Waterman, in *The Search for Excellence*, suggest eight qualities of excellent companies in the U.S. The first is a *basis for action*, which is defined as "the tendency to act, rather than to remain passive. Chaotic action is preferable to orderly inaction." Excellent companies invest time and money in experimentation and are not afraid to try. Mediocre companies, on the other hand, prefer analysis and debate; they become paralyzed by fear of failure or change.

James says, "Faith without works is useless" (James 2:20, *NASB*). When wine was needed at a wedding at Cana of Galilee, Mary told the servants concerning Jesus, "Whatever he says to you, do it" (John 2:5, *NKJV*). The sports company, Nike, borrowed its slogan, "Just Do It," from Mary. Some people are always talking about what they are going to do, but success follows action.

I heard that there are three kinds of business people: successful, unsuccessful and those giving seminars to tell the second group how the first group did it.

My favorite scene in *Star Wars* is when Luke Skywalker meets Yoda, the Jedi Master. Yoda is teaching Luke how to master the Force. Luke is using the force to lift his aircraft from the quagmire of the swamp where he crashed it, landing on Yoda's home planet. Luke succeeded in starting to lift the plane, then he lost his focus and it sank back into the muck. Frustrated, he shouts at Yoda, "I'm trying." Yoda responds, "There is no try; only do."

When people tell me they are trying to do something, I ask them, "Which is it: Are you trying to do something? Or are you doing it?" There is a world of difference between *trying to do something* and *accomplishing something*.

Our family vacations have always had a slight level of tension. Barbie likes to see things, while the kids and I like to do things. I must say she has gotten a lot better over the years. She's into sightseeing, while I'm into "sightdoing."

On our 25th anniversary trip to Hawaii, we did a lot of things and only had to see a few things. The only bad day was when she got me to go to the Polynesian culture center for the luau. We arrived just after lunch. She told me we were going to see the authentic culture of the islands. As I laid our money on the counter to get our tickets, I replied, "Honey. It's a theme park. How authentic can a theme park be?"

We went on a slow-moving canal boat around the park with a screaming child. Then we poked around displays of parts of the islands, which all looked the same, and for hours drifted in and out of shops that all contained the same trinkets. Finally, it came time for the luau, which was about the time I nearly slipped into a coma from boredom. The show was good. The meal left me starving. Then, we had to wait another hour for the evening show, going in and out of those shops. We sat on the second row. The dancers were great, very talented, but I have never heard so many loud drums since I attended a good old-fashioned rock concert.

I tried to be a good husband and endure it with her, but I have to admit I fell dead asleep during the first half of the show. So I went outside to walk around, got a Coke and came back to endure the second half. To my surprise, when I came walking back down the aisle, Barbie was on her way out. She said, "Let's go. I've seen enough." I lied and said, "Let's stay for the whole show. We came here to see the show for you." Even she had had enough. We were exhausted driving all the way back across the island of Oahu to get to our hotel. Seeing is always more exhausting than doing!

#7 ASSERTIVENESS

God gave two messages: First, "Your territory will extend." That gave Joshua vision. Second, "No one will be able to stand up against you all the days of your life." That gave him confidence. Joshua would face opposition, challenges and battles. God did not tell him that no one would oppose him, but that they would not succeed in their opposition. We confuse God's promise of victory with not ever having to face any battles.

Joshua was a warrior. Successful people have the spirit of a warrior. They know how to fight a battle and achieve victory. I don't mean to fight and strive with others, but with the challenges of life.

You will have to fight for the fulfillment of your dreams. You will face the enemies of fear, opposition and adversity. Jesus said the violent take the kingdom by force (Matthew 11:12). You will have to fight through discouragement of people who are jealous of you—who want to detour you. You will even fight spiritual battles (see Ephesians 6:10-13). So often I hear people talk about spiritual warfare, especially when they are going through a tough time. But it is always in the defensive mode. "We are undergoing spiritual attack," people say.

Let me ask you when you are going to wage spiritual warfare on the offensive? Fight the good fight and attack every spiritual enemy you are facing through prayer and faith.

#8 ADJUSTMENT

Let's look again at the statement, "No one will be able to stand up against you" (Joshua 1:5). God was telling Joshua to be flexible . . . roll with the punches . . . bounce back from his setbacks.

Joshua would have to make many adjustments throughout the campaign. Fantasy thinking wants guarantees. Fantasy thinking says, "I can't believe this is happening to me." Fantasy thinking believes that in the will of God, there are no challenges. But even Jesus faced rejection and heard a mob cry, "Crucify Him!"

Our basic coping mechanism for handling adversity is the ability to adjust to circumstances. When we can no longer adjust, our coping mechanism fails and feelings of anxiety, grief and depression take over.

One woman said, "My son is into extreme sports. My daughter is into extreme makeovers. My husband is into extreme denial."

Bill Gates says, "Success is a lousy teacher. When we win, we tend to extend the celebration as long as possible. Losing, however, gets our attention."

- You'll never be an Abraham without a sacrifice to offer.

- You'll never be a Joseph without an Egyptian dungeon to endure.

- You'll never be a Moses without a Red Sea to cross.

- You'll never be a Joshua without a Jericho to conquer.

- You'll never be a Caleb without a mountain to possess.

- You'll never be a David without a Goliath to defeat.

- You'll never be a Daniel without a night in a lion's den.

- You'll never be like Shadrach, Meshach or Abednego without a fiery furnace.

- You'll never be like Christ without a cross to carry.

- You'll never be an apostle Paul without a thorn in the flesh.

Now for the good news!

- For every sacrifice, God provides a ram in the thicket.

- For every Egyptian dungeon, God provides a throne of exaltation.

- For every Red Sea, God provides a miracle crossing.

- For every Jericho, God brings the walls tumbling down.

- For every mountain to conquer, God makes all things possible.

- For every Goliath, God gives an anointed stone in the slingshot of faith.

- For every lion's den, God provides angelic assistance.

- For every fiery furnace, God sends the fourth man in the fire.

- For every cross, God gives a resurrection to new life.

- For every thorn in the flesh, God gives all-sufficient grace!

#9 ASSOCIATION

We need to associate with visionary people. Joshua was Moses' aide. God told him, "As I was with Moses, so I will be with you" (Joshua 1:5). When we associate with spiritual people, we can see God work in their lives. We know their stories of faith and can identify with them. We can associate with people by studying the Biblical stories of faith and by studying great men and women throughout history. What made them great? How did they handle failure? What do they teach us about faith? What lessons did they leave us?

Joshua was not there when Moses grew up in Pharaoh's court, or with him when he faced Pharaoh in his court, but he knew the stories. I'm sure he asked Moses over and over to tell him how God appeared to him at the burning bush, and what it was like to have seen the back side of God on Mount Sinai when he prayed, "Lord, show me your glory." There is no doubt that the success of Joshua was directly connected with his close, personal association with Moses.

#10 ASSURANCE

Three times God tells Joshua, "Be strong and very courageous." Why? "For the Lord your God will be with you wherever you go" (Joshua 1:9). It takes faith to turn dreams into reality. Joshua trusted God to win the battles they faced and to lead the people to victory. God told him, "I will never leave you nor forsake you" (Joshua 1:5).

You can face anything with the presence of the Lord. Here is God's promise to you: "My Presence will go with you and I will give you rest" (Exodus 33:14). The last words Jesus spoke while on earth were these: "I am with you always, even to the end of the age" (Matthew 28:20).

Joshua put the Lord first and foremost. He fulfilled his mission as a calling from God. His final affirmation of faith was, "As for me and my house, we will serve the Lord" (Joshua 24:15, *NKJV*).

All truly successful people trust God and give Him glory for all their accomplishments. Successful people also motivate others to develop their spiritual life by following the Lord just as Joshua did. He told the leaders of Israel to make a spiritual commitment: "Choose you this day whom you will serve." He knew of no success that did not put God at the center of his endeavors.

When President Kennedy was assassinated in Dallas, Texas, he was there to deliver a speech. In his speech, he planned to quote the words of Jesus: "What shall it profit a man if he gains the whole world and loses his own soul?"

HEALTHY
RELATIONSHIPS

John Donne wrote: "No man is an island, entire of itself." From the moment we are born, we are engaged in a world of relationships. Or should I say, entangled in a web of relationships. Our survival depends totally on our relationship to our parents when we are born. Relationships shape and mold our personalities. We are shaped by our friendships, peers, colleagues, spouse, family, work, community, politics and church.

We are who we are, primarily because of the relationships that have influenced us and continue to influence us. Our relationships have helped to shape our attitudes, values, beliefs, philosophy of life, world view and lifestyle.

God created us for relationships. The first thing He said about Adam was, "It is not good for the man to be alone" (Genesis 2:18). Or, maybe the first thing He said was, "I can do better than that." So He created Eve! In either case, He made a partner for Adam and the human story began with a relationship.

Jesus summed up real spirituality in terms of relationships in the greatest commandments: love God, love others and love yourself. Our success and level of happiness depends largely on the quality of our relationships. We struggle to manage our relationships. Perhaps no relationship is undergoing more stress in our culture today than marriage.

A couple, both 50, celebrated their 25th wedding anniversary. On their special day, a good fairy came to them and said that because they had been so devoted to one another, she would grant one wish to each of them. The wife wished for a trip around the world with her husband. Whoosh! Immediately she had cruise tickets in her hands. It was the husband's turn. He looked at his loving wife; he looked at those tickets. Then, with a devilish twinkle in his eyes, he wished for a much younger wife. And whoosh . . . he turned 75!

We hear a lot about dysfunctional, unhealthy and codependent relationships, but what are the guidelines for healthy relationships? The New Testament gives a series of principles for relationships by using the phrase *one another* in each of these passages.

#1 LOVE ONE ANOTHER

Jesus left us this charge:

> "A new command I give you: Love one another. As I have loved you, so you must love one another. By this all men will know that you are my disciples, if you love one another" (John 13:34, 35).

Our age knows little about true love.

We love if . . . you are beautiful . . . if you give me what I want . . . if you can help advance my career . . . if you meet my political agenda. *We love because of* . . .

what you can do for me . . . your fit with my plans . . . your position in life.

But divine love—the love of God in Christ—is *love in spite of . . . love*. Love that does not count the cost of investment . . . love that looks for nothing in return . . . love that is unconditional, nonjudgmental and unchanging.

Jesus sets the standard very high for love. He tells us to love as He loves us. Now, that's raising the bar. Paul said, "Be devoted to one another in brotherly love. Honor one another above yourselves" (Romans 12:10).

My two brothers and I grew up fighting and competing, so I'm not exactly sure what Paul meant by brotherly love. It doesn't sound all that spiritual to me. I think he means to love as a family. Healthy families have a deep bond of commitment that transcends conflict, tragedy and disappointment. Love can weather any storm, survive any tragedy and conquer any enemy.

Love is measured by the Cross. Love is selfless and sacrificial; it transcends the self. Jesus said, "Greater love hath no man than this, that a man lay down his life for his friends" (John 15:13, KJV). True love lays something down in order to gain something greater. The question for us is, Where is the influence of the Cross in our relationships?" A cross is only useful for one thing—an execution. We have to die to self-centeredness in order to live in love. Until we die to self, we are not free to love as Christ loves us.

You may be saying right now, "But we aren't capable of loving others like that." True. In and of ourselves, we are not capable. But Christ has given us a new heart and a new mind. He has given us the Holy Spirit who gives us the capacity to love others with divine love. "God has poured out his love in our heart by the Holy Spirit, whom He has given us" (Romans 5:5). God empowers us to love by His Spirit and Christ teaches us how to love as He loves. So we have both empowerment and education in the school of divine love.

Most of our decisions start with, "What's in it for me?" But true love asks, "How can I bring glory to God and bless others?" When we have the priorities of love in order, God will take care of our needs.

#2 AGREE WITH ONE ANOTHER

"I appeal to you . . . that all of you agree with one another so that there may be no divisions among you and that you may be perfectly united in mind and thought" (1 Corinthians 1:10). The word *agree* is *sumphanoo*, meaning "to sound together as a symphony." A symphony is based on each person playing his or her instrument in harmony with the others.

We are to be in spiritual agreement on the doctrine of Christ. We are to "contend for the faith" (Jude 3). We are never to be in agreement with any philosophical or religious system that demeans the person of Christ and makes Him less than He is—the eternal, sinless Son of God, the Savior of the world and Lord of all.

We are to agree with others in prayer, providing the prayer is according to the will of God. Jesus said, "If any two of you on earth agree about anything you ask for, it will be done for you by my Father in heaven" (Matthew 18:19). But that is not a blank check from the Almighty, leaving it up to us to fill in the blank. Two people may agree about something in prayer, yet not be in agreement with the will of God.

There are times, however, when we should not be in agreement with someone. We are not to agree about something that is wrong according to Scripture. The moral collapse of our culture has brought us to the all-time low of calling good evil and evil good. Culture may change its morality, but God's Word never changes.

We cannot agree with false doctrine. Jesus commended the Ephesian congregation because they tested those who claimed to be apostles and found them to be false (see Revelation 2:2). Many false apostles, prophets and teachers are proclaiming many messages in the name of the Lord. But they do not speak for the cause of Christ. They merely merchandise the gospel for their own profit.

We can never agree with something that is harmful or detrimental to another person. I don't mean we should mind other people's business. We should not. People are free to make their own decisions. But when we see someone with whom we have a close relationship making a poor decision, we need to talk with them and ask them to consider the consequences and to reconsider. To sit by idly and let them make a bad decision constitutes negligence on our part. Our silence is a form of endorsing what they are doing.

#3 ACCEPT ONE ANOTHER

We live in fear of rejection. We are afraid to be ourselves, thinking someone will not accept us. Ours is a world of conditional love. The magnetism of Jesus was His loving acceptance of everyone, regardless of station in life. The Christian ethic is one of unconditional acceptance: "Accept one another, then, just as Christ accepted you, in order to bring praise to God" (Romans 15:7).

Acceptance includes respect, which actually means "to behold the beauty of." *Acceptance* is unconditional, nonjudgmental love. We are to accept each other's differences and show appreciation for the uniqueness of every person. We need to abandon the mission of trying to change people to be like us. The world would be very boring if everyone was alike. God has created us with uniqueness and diversity.

The context of Paul's admonition to accept each other is the differences of personal convictions held by Christians (see Romans 14). God has enough laws stated in Scripture. We don't need any more moral laws. While each person needs to set personal convictions about issues not specifically addressed in Scripture, we are forbidden against making our convictions laws for other people to live by.

We have different opinions about issues. We should accept and respect our differences. We need an environment of grace not legalism. God's law is immutable but our personal rules are subjective and should never be used to divide the body of Christ. Legalism brings bondage. We are to search the Scriptures and pray for guidance on personal issues. The Holy Spirit will lead each of us individually. "It is for freedom that Christ has set [you] free" (Galatians 5:1).

#4 SERVE ONE ANOTHER

"You, my brothers, were called to be free. But do not use your freedom to indulge the sinful nature; rather, serve one another in love" (Galatians 5:13). The word *serve* (*douleuo*, Greek) means "to serve as a *doulos*," which is Greek for bondslave. The word *douloo* means to bring into bondage. However, the doulous is not a servant by force, but by choice. Here it is a voluntary act of the will. To bring oneself under submission to the law of love means to be a slave of love. The only motivation we need for service is love, not coercion.

The greatest portrait of Jesus, second only to the Cross, is when He washed the feet of His disciples. Because they wore sandals or went barefoot, foot washing was a common act of hospitality in the ancient world. Typically, people washed their own feet when they entered someone's home. If a person was wealthy, he could afford a servant who would wash the feet of his guests. Jesus assumed the place of a servant when He washed the disciples' feet.

The real question is *why* He performed such an act of service. It was because the disciples were arguing around the Passover table about who was the most important among them (see Luke 22). So, to teach them about real greatness in the kingdom of God and what spiritual leadership really meant, He performed a simple act of service. Then He challenged them: "Now that I, your Lord and Teacher have washed your feet, you also should wash one another's feet. I have set you an example that you should do as I have done for you" (John 13:14, 15). They were blown away by His actions and they learned their lesson that night about the dangers of vying for power, when they should be serving one another in love.

I don't know how much power and authority you have. Perhaps you have been given great influence and power, but I know you will agree with me when I say your power does not rival the power of Jesus. He has all power in heaven and on earth. So, if the One who has all power is willing to wash our feet and to serve us in love, what does that say to us about how we are to use the power and authority He has entrusted to us?

#5 CARRY ONE ANOTHER'S BURDENS

"Carry each other's burdens, and in this way you will fulfill the law of Christ . . . each one should carry his own load" (Galatians 6:2, 5). How do we reconcile these two statements? The word *carry* (*bastazo*, Greek) means "to support as a burden." Christ carried the cross, the burden of our sins and guilt. He bore our sins in His body on the tree (1 Peter 2:24). "Surely he has borne our griefs and carried our sorrows," the prophet foretold (Isaiah 53:4, *NKJV*). The cross is a symbol of a burden Christ commands us to carry. "And anyone who does not carry his cross and follow me cannot be my disciple" (Luke 14:27). One of the ways we carry the cross is to get involved in the sufferings of others, even as Christ identified Himself with our sin and suffering.

We are responsible *to* each other, but we are not responsible *for* each other. Ours is the age of victimization, where many people refuse to assume responsibility for their actions. Carrying each other's burdens is balanced out by the challenge, "Each one should carry his own load." We are to carry each other's burdens only when someone is incapable of doing so. Get them on their feet, and then they can take responsibility for their lives. We are to teach people how to carry the load of life.

Such is the picture of the Good Samaritan who band-aged the man's wounds, put him on his own donkey and took him to the inn. He paid the hotel bill. Then he went back to check on him until he was well and back on his feet, but he did not get into a codependent relationship with the injured man. Now maybe they stayed in contact by e-mail. You can carry the story out as long as you like. But one thing's for sure—the wounded man didn't stay indefinitely in the hotel, living on room service!

Codependency means that both parties are getting something out of the relationship that is dysfunctional. One *helps* the other, who gets the emotional and financial benefits, while the helper gets the emotional return of feeling important and needed. The one being helped is stuck in a place of always depending on others instead of growing to maturity. There is a difference between helping and enabling someone to stay in their condition. What is maturity? It means being strong enough to carry your own load. We are to carry someone's burden only until they are able to carry their own load and take charge of their own life.

#6 BUILD ONE ANOTHER UP

I find this statement to be one of the most challenging statements in the Bible:

Do not let any unwholesome talk come out of your mouths, but only what is helpful for building others up according to their needs, that it may benefit those who listen (Ephesians 4:29).

The word *oikodemo*, means "to build a house" (*oikos*, a house; *domeo*, to build [Romans 14:19; 1 Corinthians 8:2, 14:12; 2 Corinthians 10:8; Ephesians 4:12]). The concept of building involves the slow progress that results from patient effort. I will tell you two things about building a house. First, it will take longer than you think. Second, it will cost more than you plan.

The same is true with building up people. When we minister to others to help build them up, it will take longer than we think and cost more than we realize. But we need to make the commitment to build them into the persons God created them to be.

Fathers are told to build their children up, never to put them down (Ephesians 6:4). Things grow in an upward direction. Words of faith, hope and love build up. "Each one should please his neighbor for his own good, to build him up" (Romans 15:2). Paul spoke of the "authority the Lord gave us for building you up rather than pulling you down" (2 Corinthians 10:8). He also challenged us to "excel in gifts that build up the church" (1 Corinthians 14:12).

The Pygmalion Phenomenon is a psychological term for giving a person a positive self-image that will motivate them to achieve it. The story of *My Fair Lady* is based on this principle. The Pygmalion Phenomenon states that when we describe people, based on their future potential, rather than their current state, they will rise to the level of that potential. If, however, our vision is limited to their current condition, and we only describe them as they are, or worse, show no confidence in their potential, their growth will be limited. When they internalize our negative view of them, they remain the same.

For this reason, I am opposed to labels and stereotypes. If you accept negative labels about yourself or adhere to stereotypes instead of being the unique person you are, you will limit your potential.

God has given us the only labels we need in Scripture. We are sons and daughters of God, heirs of God and coheirs with Christ, redeemed by His love, empowered by His Spirit, and we are the people of God!

Jesus saw a ragtag group of fishermen and said, "Come, follow me . . . and I will make you fishers of men" (Matthew 4:19). Until that moment, they never dreamed of doing anything but catching, cleaning and selling fish in Capernaum. But Jesus gave them a new vision for life, and they rose to a higher level. They not only believed in Him, they also discovered that He believed in them. In return, they started to believe in themselves. They achieved a higher level of success for the kingdom of God than they ever dreamed possible because of the way Jesus built them up. He inspired them to greatness because He knew how to build them up.

I am confident that you believe in God, but it is time you realize that He believes in you and He has endowed you with gifts, talents and abilities. "If God be for [you], who can be against [you]?" (Romans 8:31, *NKJV*).

#7 SUBMIT TO ONE ANOTHER

One of the most important principles for success is the law of submission. "Submit to one another out of reverence for Christ" (Ephesians 5:21). We struggle with this law because it runs contrary to our nature. Typically, we think of success in terms of being aggressive, assertive, climbing to the top of the ladder, winning at all costs and the survival of the fittest. But in the Kingdom, the way up is the way down. The way to the top is the way of submission and humility.

Paul shows us how the principle of submission is to be applied in all relationships of life. Well, what is submission? The word *submit (hupostasso,* Greek) means "to come under the authority of another, or to come under to support." It is a military word used to describe troops that stand together, arrayed for battle. Paul uses the word 23 times in his writings to describe Christian relationships.

Submission means "servanthood." It is the opposite of asserting one's rights or demanding one's way. It is the opposite of an independent, autocratic spirit that fails to take into consideration the needs and desires of others. Submission is not forced by another, but it is the act of one's own free will as an expression of love. *Submission* is a mark of maturity and the key to peace. "The wisdom that comes from heaven is . . . submissive. . . . Peacemakers who sow in peace, raise a harvest of righteousness" (James 3:17, 18).

Some people are more prone to submission than others. An 8-year-old's essay on Quakers read as follows: "Quakers are very meek, quiet people who never fight or argue back. My father is a Quaker, but my mother is something else."

#8 BEAR WITH ONE ANOTHER

The word *bear* is quite descriptive. "Bear with each other and forgive whatever grievances you may have against one other. Forgive as the Lord forgave you" (Colossians 3:13).

Have you ever been sharing with someone or a group and said, "Bear with me for a moment?" You were asking them to give you time to express yourself. You were asking them to be patient with you.

The Greek word is *anecho*, meaning "to hold up, to endure, to tolerate." The noun form of the word means "to hold back," as God holds back the day of judgment; and it gives us mercy and space to repent. God overlooked the sins of the past because He was looking forward to the day of atonement on the cross (Romans 3:25).

We are to be patient in the moment because we can see people's future potential. "Be completely humble and gentle; be patient, bearing with one another in love" (Ephesians 4:2). We have to be able to see people's future potential and nurture that potential instead of overreacting to everything they do wrong in the present. To forgive means to overlook the offense in the hope and expectation of future blessings. On the cross Jesus prayed, "Father, forgive them for they know not what they do."

We don't have to overreact to the wrongs people do to us. "A man's wisdom gives him patience; it is to his glory to overlook an offense" (Proverbs 19:11). Instead of judging one another, and broadcasting everybody's sins, we need to heed the counsel of the apostle Peter: "Above all, love each other deeply, because love covers over a multitude of sins" (1 Peter 4:8).

#9 ENCOURAGE ONE ANOTHER

Everyone needs encouragement.

> And let us consider how we may spur one another on toward love and good deeds. Let us not give up meeting together, as some are in the habit of doing, but let us encourage one another—and all the more as you see the Day approaching (Hebrews 10:24, 25).

To *spur* (*paroxusmos*, Greek) means "to incite, irritate or exasperate." The fact that the writer uses a negative word in a positive way makes the point even more striking. We are to encourage, which means to impart courage and faith.

Are you making a positive impact on your friends and family? Are you spurring others on toward love and good deeds? Who is more active in prayer and service because of your influence on them? Are you an instrument of faith, or are you like the 10 spies of ancient Israel who cause the hearts of the people to melt with fear because they brought back a bad report about giants in the Promised Land?

What a tragedy to see people of faith speak words of doubt and fear every time they face a challenge. We are people of faith. We face every challenge of life with faith that believes, "With God all things are possible" (Matthew 19:26).

Encouragement is one of the reasons we gather for worship. We are to encourage each other more and more as the day of Christ's return draws near. When we think about the promise of Christ's return, we are to "encourage each other with these words" (1 Thessalonians 4:18). The Scripture itself is given to encourage us (see Romans 15:4).

The Greek word *encourage* is *parakaleo*, from the words *para* (beside, near) and *kaleo* (call). It implies actually being with someone to reassure and encourage them. This is the name Jesus gave the Holy Spirit, the Comforter, the Paraklete (John 14:16). Barnabas was called the Son of Encouragement by the apostle (Acts 4:36). *Encouragement* is the one ministry every person is called to and something every person can get involved in. Go out every day on a mission to encourage others in their faith.

#10 PRAY FOR ONE ANOTHER

"Therefore confess you sins to each other and pray for each other so that you may be healed" (James 5:16). Prayer is directly connected with healing—spiritually, emotionally, physically and relationally. Prayer is one of the greatest gifts we can give each other. Our attitude towards people changes when we pray for them. God's power is released in people's lives and situations when we pray for them.

POWERFUL
PRAYER

Have you heard the new universal prayer? "So far today, God, I've done all right. I haven't gossiped. I haven't lost my temper. I haven't been greedy, grumpy, nasty or self-centered. I'm really glad about that. But in a few minutes God, I'm going to need a lot of help . . . because I'm going to get out of bed!"

A father explained Newton's law of gravity to his son and how it holds things together. His son asked, "Well, Dad, how did things hold together before they passed this law?"

We don't pass the laws that govern life, we discover them. They are God's laws, woven into the fabric of the cosmos itself.

Just as the law of gravity holds our lives together, the law of prayer holds us together spiritually. Life is filled with mysteries. We know certain things work, and we enjoy them, but we are mystified by not knowing exactly how or why they work. Yet, we trust these laws of life and laws of science because they make our lives better. So it is with prayer. We experience the power and benefits of prayer, yet we remain baffled as to how prayer works.

What is prayer? Prayer is talking and listening to God. It takes on many expressions: thanksgiving, confession, petition, intercession and dedication. While I don't fully understand everything there is to the science of prayer, one thing I do know: *Prayer works!* In fact, the power of prayer has been confirmed by research. People who pray experience a relief from stress and a greater sense of peace; recover better from illness; possess a greater sense of purpose and meaning (connectedness); have greater marital satisfaction; enjoy a sense of fulfillment; and are more likely to forgive others.

One day the disciples were with Jesus while He was praying. They said, "Lord, teach us to pray." Thinking He would give them some new heavenly insights, He repeated what He taught early on in His ministry, what we call the Lord's Prayer. Never do we hear them say to Him, "Teach us to preach, or teach us to worship or teach us to minister," although He did teach them these things. They saw the connection between His praying and His power.

Prayer was essential to Christ: He modeled the priority of prayer. Even though He was divine, He prayed. Even though He worked miracles, He prayed. Even though He was Lord of all, He prayed. Prayer was His habit. "Very early, while it was still dark, Jesus got up, left the house and went off to a solitary place where he prayed" (Mark 1:35). He prayed all night before choosing the Twelve. He prayed before he broke the bread and fish and fed the multitude. He prayed before he raised Lazarus from the dead. He prayed before he went to the cross. He prayed from the cross, "Father forgive them for they know not what they are doing."

Jesus gives us a strategy for prayer. The Lord's Prayer covers every aspect of life. It is not only a model for prayer, it is a model for life. The way we pray determines how we live, and the way we live determines how we pray.

#1 RELATIONSHIP

"Our Father." Prayer is more than ritual, liturgy or poetry; *prayer* is a dynamic relationship with God as our Father, with Christ as our Intercessor, and the Holy Spirit as our Helper. The fatherhood of God means that He is the source of life. What kind of Father is God? Jesus spoke of God in such relational terms. Many in His day thought of God as Lawgiver, Judge, Creator or Redeemer. But Father? Jesus modeled a close, personal relationship with the heavenly Father and He taught us to think of God as our Father.

In one sense of the word, we all call God our Father in Creation. Yet, sin estranges us from God. Jesus came to save us from sin and to reconcile us to the Father. Some people have difficulty relating to God as Father. The concept of a father is associated with pain. They think of the abusive father or the negligent father. But we don't measure the fatherhood of God by our imperfect fathers.

A Sunday school teacher noticed little Johnny drawing a picture of an old man. "Who's picture are you drawing?" she asked.

"I'm drawing a picture of God," he said assuredly.

"But no one has ever seen God. No one knows what God looks like," the teacher told him.

Johnny said, "Well, they will when I finish this picture."

Jesus showed us what God really looks like. God is love and He cares for us as a gentle, yet powerful, Father.

#2 REALITY

The secular man can see no higher than the earth. His sense of reality is limited to what he can see naturally. Yet, Jesus said we are to pray, "Our Father, who art in heaven." The worship of Gaia, Mother Earth, is a New Age fad. Such a vision of life can see no higher than the earth, soil or matter. We are earth bound, according to the secularist. We come from the earth and return to it. But faith sees the reality of heaven. Ecclesiastes says the body returns to the ground from which it came and the spirit returns to the God who gave it.

The Bible uses the term *heaven* in three ways: the atmosphere, the spiritual realm and the dwelling of God. Jesus spoke of heaven over 100 times in the Gospels. Reality is more than time, space and matter. The universe came into being out of nothing. "By faith we understand that the universe was formed at God's command, so that what is seen was not made out of what was visible" (Hebrews 11:3).

In fact, what we call matter is mostly perceived rays of light. Your body is 75 percent water, and every atom in your body is separated from the other by empty space. Yet you appear to be a solid mass because your eyes interpret rays of light. Heaven means God is sovereign. He is in control of earth's affairs and of history. "The Lord has established his throne in heaven" (Psalm 103:19).

Jesus described heaven as a place of perfection. "In my Father's house there are many dwelling places . . .

I go to prepare a place for you" (John 14:2, 3, *NASB*). John was translated to heaven, saw things to come and wrote about the celestial city in the Revelation. Life looks different from the vantage point of heaven.

#3 REVERENCE

An interviewer asked a comedian who starred in a weekly comedy, "What has made your television show such a big success?"

He responded, "Our program is successful because we consider absolutely nothing sacred."

Have we entered a time in American history when absolutely nothing is sacred? Jesus teaches us to pray, "Hallowed by thy name."

We can identify with the prophet Daniel who was exiled to Babylon during the Jewish captivity. One evening Belshazzar, king of Babylon, hosted a royal party. When the party reached its peak of debauchery, he ordered the holy articles used in the Jewish temple for worship be brought out so the attendees could eat and drink from the sacred vessels. He profaned the holy vessels and experienced God's judgment. He, too, considered absolutely nothing sacred. The party ended abruptly when the hand of God appeared, writing a mysterious message on the palace wall: *Mene Mene Tekel, Uparsin*. None of the king's wise men could interpret it. So Daniel was brought in to do the task. His interpretation pronounced God's judgment against Babylon: *Mene:* God has numbered the days of your reign and brought it to an end. *Tekel:* You have been weighed on the scales and found wanting. *Uparsin:* Your kingdom is divided and given to the Medes and Persians.

Shortly after seeing the handwriting on the wall, Belshazzar's kingdom fell at the invasion of the Medes and Persians. For Belshazzar, nothing was sacred. We need to recapture a sense of awe about those things that are sacred. God instructed the Levitical priests to "distinguish between the holy and the profane, between the unclean and the clean" (Leviticus 10:10, *NASB*). So must we.

The third commandment tells us not to misuse God's name but to revere it. What does it mean to misuse God's name or to take God's name in vain? The name of God describes who He is, His essential nature, character and person. The ancient Hebrews thought of a name as the representation of a person. The Hebrew word translated *misuse* or *take in vain* means "to lift up and attach it to emptiness." It means to rob God of His majesty, to reduce our thoughts of Him to the realm of the commonplace, and to exclude Him from our lives.

The name of God and the name of Jesus have become common swear words in our culture. The word *profanity* comes from two Latin words, *pro* meaning "in front of," and *fane*, meaning "temple." A profane word, then, is a word one would not use in a temple or in a church. We need a revival of personal and national reverence for God.

#4 RESIGNATION

The goal of prayer is not to get God to meet our agenda, but to align ourselves with His agenda. Jesus teaches us to pray, "Thy kingdom come, thy will be done." These two phrases echo each other.

The kingdom of God is the rule of God. Christ came to bring us into the Kingdom and to establish the Kingdom in us. God created us with a will, and most of us have a strong will! God does not want to destroy the human will. We hear about God breaking the will. God does not want to break our will but to bend it and mold it in submission to His will and plan. God wants us to submit our wills to Him so that we exercise our wills in ways that benefit us and others.

Parents train their children to think for themselves and to make good decisions. Children have to learn to obey authority first before they can exercise their wills properly. Without obedience being learned, we tend toward rebellion. James tells us to put all our plans in submission to the will of God. "Instead, you ought to say, 'If it is the Lord's will we live and do this or that'" (4:15).

#5 REQUEST

The most basic definition of prayer is to ask God for something. Jesus taught us to tell God our needs and ask Him for help and provision: "Give us today our daily bread." We never want to take God's blessings for granted. We never want to start thinking that we are producing everything by ourselves. "Every good and perfect gift is from above" (James 1:17).

When we ask God for what we need, we are depending on Him. "It is He who gives you the ability to produce wealth" (Deuteronomy 8:18). Remember, "In him we live, and move and have our being" (Acts 17:28). We live *in Him*. We don't merely live in the atmosphere or in the political climate, or in the economic system or in the convenience of science and technology. But *in Him!* He is the source of all things. "For from Him and through Him and to Him are all things" (Romans 11:36).

I once read that there is nothing too great for God's power and nothing too small for His Fatherly care. Pray about everything! Don't miss out on something because you failed to ask God for it. James tells us, "You do not have because you do not ask God" (James 4:2).

I have a close friend who is a financial planner. One of his catch phrases is, "Don't leave any money on the table." Well, don't leave any blessings on the table by failing to ask God. Take Jesus' counsel to heart: "Ask and it will be given to you, seek and you will find; knock and the door will be opened to you" (Matthew 7:7).

#6 REPENTANCE

We are to pray, "Forgive us our debts." Christ saves us from the penalty and power of sin. Yet, "we all stumble in many ways" (James 3:2). When we sin, we need to confess our sins and repent, which means to have a change of mind. We need to see moral issues from the standpoint of God's truth found in Scripture. Human nature tends to rationalize and justify sin. When we see things God's way, we will live accordingly.

After graduating college, I began my preaching ministry in Southern California. I preached a sermon on holiness as a revival speaker for a church. After the service, the pastor told me he appreciated my sermon on holiness except for one thing. He disagreed with my point that holiness is an ongoing process of spiritual development in a Christian's life. "I believe in entire sanctification," he said. "In fact, when I was young I responded to an altar call in service. When I went forward, people prayed for me and I was completely sanctified." Then he added, (which blew my mind), "Since that night I have never committed a sin. But, I have made a few mistakes." Well, call it what you will, sins or mistakes—we aren't perfect.

#7 RECONCILIATION:

When we ask God to forgive us, we are to forgive those who have wronged us. This is the only part of the prayer Jesus expounds on in His Sermon on the Mount. "For if you forgive men when they sin against you, your heavenly Father will also forgive you. But if you do not forgive men their sins, your Father will not forgive your sins" (Matthew 6:14, 15).

Kim Phuc Phan Thi was only 9 years old when her village was bombed with napalm during the Vietnam war. She is the little girl in the famous war photo of Vietnam who was running down the street when the bombs were dropped. Her clothes were burned off by the napalm, and much of her body disfigured. She endured 17 surgeries and years of physical rehabilitation. Today she is married, has two sons, and is an outspoken witness for Jesus Christ.

In my interview with Kim, I asked her this question: "What is the single most important lesson you have learned from your experience?"

She replied, "I learned how much God loves me and that He gave His Son to die on the cross for my sins. If God loves me so much and has forgiven me, then I can forgive my enemies. I learned from Jesus to love my enemies. As I prayed for my enemies, the anger left my heart. My heart became soft the more I prayed for them. Finally, I was free because I forgave them."

#8 REINFORCEMENT

Jesus taught us to pray, "Lead us not into temptation." Temptation is no respecter of persons. "No temptation has seized you except what is common to man" (1 Corinthians 10:13).

A minister was late for an appointment downtown. He drove around for 15 minutes looking for a parking space. When he couldn't find one, he decided to park in a handicap space. He left a note on the windshield in case a policeman caught him: "I have been a minister in this city for 20 years. I am late for an appointment. This is the only space I could find. Forgive us our trespasses." And he signed it.

When he came out of his meeting, he found a traffic ticket on his windshield with a note attached: "I have been a police officer in this city for the past 20 years. I must give you this ticket. Lead us not into temptation."

God will not lead us into temptation. This part of the prayer means, "Father, do not allow us to be overcome with temptation. Keep us alert and strong in the face of temptation. Give us the grace to say no to temptation and yes to Your will."

Prayer makes us spiritually strong to face temptation. Paul tells us we are in a spiritual war against the powers of darkness, so we are to be strong in the Lord (see Ephesians 6:10). How can we be strong? By prayer. "And pray in the Spirit on all occasions with all kinds of prayers and requests. With this in mind, be alert and always keep on praying for all saints" (v. 18).

We yield to temptation because we have areas of spiritual weakness. Jesus told the disciples in Gethsemane, "Watch and pray so that you will not fall into temptation. The spirit is willing, but the body is weak"

(Matthew 26:41). We are attacked at our point of weakness by fear, lust, greed, power and selfishness. We all have an Achilles heel. We fall into sin when we get careless.

To be tempted means to be seduced, distracted, led off course. Fishermen use bait to catch the attention of a fish. The fish is swimming in a straight line when suddenly it notices the movement of the bait. It is drawn off course, snatches the enticing bait and end of story!

The power of prayer makes us discerning of temptation and gives us strength against its enticement so that we are not deceived and destroyed by it. Eskimos use a deceptive hunting device to kill wolves, bears and other prey. They take a long sliver of whale bone and sharpen its edges like the points of a dagger. Then they soften it until it becomes pliable enough to be bent into the form of a barb. Frozen in this coiled position and embedded in a piece of meat, it is set as a trap for the prey. The hungry animal consumes the bait, not knowing it will mean his death. The warmth of the animal's body thaws the barb, which pierces his stomach. Slowly, painfully he bleeds to death by the blade he cannot see, cannot identify and cannot dislodge. He never even associates his pain with the delicious meat he ate some time earlier.

#9 RESISTANCE

We are to pray, "Deliver us from evil." Actually, this means "from the Evil One." *Evil* is personified in Scripture as the devil. He is the enemy of humanity. While we may not see this being called the devil, we are certainly aware of his diabolical presence in the world. Although we live in the age of reason with science and technology as the order of the day, the problem of evil is very real. The occult occupies a major place in the world—even in America! Some people think of Satan as a personality, while others see Satan as the force of evil.

Prayer is one of the keys in resisting the devil. "Resist the devil, and he will flee from you." How? "Draw near to God" (James 4:7, 8). The Reformer Martin Luther said the best way to resist the devil is to ignore him. He can't stand to be ignored.

George Muller Massena, one of Napoleon's generals, suddenly appeared with 18,000 soldiers before an Austrian town that had no means of defending itself. The town council met, certain that capitulation was the only answer. The old dean of the church reminded the council that it was Easter, and begged them to hold services as usual and leave the trouble in God's hands. They followed his advice. The dean went to the church and rang the bells to announce the service. Hearing church bells, the French soldiers concluded that the Austrian army had come to rescue the town. They broke camp, and vanished before the bells had ceased ringing.

#10 RECOGNITION

Prayer leads us to a victorious philosophy of life: "Thine is the kingdom, the power, and the glory." *Humanism* places man at the center of all things and asserts that man is the measure of all things. But we know that the Almighty God is the measure of all things.

Here are three great realities of life:

God's kingdom is the only lasting kingdom. The cosmos, with its billions of stars and galaxies are His, and He calls them all by name. He reigns omnipotent over all! The kingdoms of man come and go, but His kingdom is an eternal kingdom. "Since we are receiving a kingdom that cannot be shaken, let us be thankful" (Hebrews 12:28).

God has all power in the universe. Any power we harness is a gift from the Creator. All power belongs to God. Any personal power He gives us is an entrusted responsibility to serve others. "Power belongs to God" (Psalm 62:11, *NKJV*). So we can trust His power to be sufficient for every need.

God deserves all the glory. The ultimate purpose of life is to bring glory to God. "Not to us, O Lord, not to us but to your name be the glory, because of your love and faithfulness" (Psalm 115:1). One day we will face the Lord of eternity and hear him say to us: "Well done, good and faithful servant" (Matthew 25:21).

The great missionary Hudson Taylor, who founded the Overseas Missionary Fellowship, gave this excellent advice: "Let us give up our work, our plans, ourselves, our lives, our loved ones, our influence, our all, right into [God's] hand; and then, when we have given all over to Him, there will be nothing left for us to be troubled about."

Dynamic Decisions

The adage goes, "Life is a game of chance." In reality, life is a game of choice. Our choices have far more to do with our standard of living than does chance or circumstance. Accepting the freedom and responsibility for our choices empowers us to take charge of our lives so that we live as victors, rather than victims.

At the end of Joshua's life, he gathered the leaders of Israel together at Shechem. He issued a charge for the them to make a life-changing decision that would impact generations to come. "Choose you this day whom you will serve." He then declared his personal choice: "As for me and my house we will serve the Lord" (Joshua 24:15, *NKJV*). The leaders responded, "We also will serve the Lord" (v. 18). Joshua made a God-centered choice that had implications for his whole life. What I mean by godly decisions are decisions that put God and His will at the center of our lives, instead of on the periphery.

Every day we make decisions—small ones and big ones, significant ones and insignificant ones. Decision determines destiny. Our destiny is not predetermined. We determine our destiny every day by the choices we make.

Moses said, "I have set before you life and death . . . now choose life that you and your children may live" (Deuteronomy 30:19).

Elijah asked his generation: "How long will you waver between two opinions? If the Lord is God, follow Him; but if Baal (a false god of Canaan) is God, then follow him" (1 Kings 18:21).

When Daniel was carried into exile in Babylon, he made a quality decision that he was not going to be absorbed into the culture. Daniel "resolved not to defile himself" (Daniel 1:8). He was shaped by his inner choice, not by cultural forces around him.

Jesus said, "If anyone chooses to do God's will, he will find out whether my teaching comes from God or whether I speak on my own" (John 7:17).

The greatest choice every person makes is not who to marry, what college to attend, what career to pursue or what house to buy. The greatest choice is to follow Jesus Christ as Lord. When we make the decision to follow Him, we pass from death unto life and all things become new.

Sometimes we want to blame others, or even God for our choices. I find this often in marriage counseling when couples are having trouble. They use a lot of "God-talk" and say that God brought them together (implying that God got them into their current predicament). I remind them that God did not force them to marry. He didn't push them down the aisle of the church and coerce them into saying their vows. They got married because they chose to get married. That comes as a startling revelation to many couples.

Walking down the street one day, a woman heard a voice yell, "Stop! If you take another step, you will be killed!" She froze in her tracks. Seconds later, a brick fell from a building and landed in her path. A minute or two after that, she was getting ready to cross the street when the same voice bellowed, "Stop! Don't cross the street now!" An out-of-control truck sped around the corner and didn't even slow down as it ran the red light. Shaken, the woman asked out loud, "Who are you?"

"I am your guardian angel," the voice replied. "I imagine you have some questions for me," said the angel.

"You bet I do," the woman said. "Where were you on my wedding day?"

Here are 10 ways to make decisions that count.

#1 CHOOSE THE LONG-RANGE OVER THE SHORT-RANGE

When making a big decision, ask yourself, "Where will this lead me?" All significant decisions have long-range results. Many mistakes are made because of shortsighted thinking. You need a vision for life that is long-range. Project into the future and see where your decision today will ultimately lead.

All actions have reactions. All causes produce effects. Decisions have results and consequences. The law of sowing and reaping is important to understand (see Galatians 6:7-9).

Jesus is the most courageous person who ever lived. He faced the cross by His own choice to obtain our eternal salvation. One of the most powerful statements about Jesus is found in Hebrews 12:2, "For the joy set before him endured the cross, scorning its shame, and sat down at the right hand of the throne of God." He went from the sufferings of the cross to the glories of the throne because He chose the long-range over the short-range.

#2 CHOOSE A NEW WAY

Remember this powerful principle: *What was once decided can be undecided.* Don't get trapped by your conditioned behavior or your traditions. If life is not working for you, change your strategy! Change your mindset! Change your . . .

- Traditions that keep you trapped.

- Conditioned behaviors that are unproductive.

- Life-strategy that isn't working.

- Programmed thinking that is isn't true.

Now I do not mean truths stated in Scripture. God's Word never changes. But we grow up believing some things are in the Bible or that they are right, when actually they are not even addressed in Scripture. We are programmed with fear and guilt, so we never change, even though we want to. Until you change your thinking about something, you can't change the way you live. You are only transformed by "the renewing our your mind" (Romans 12:2).

Jesus called for new thinking. "No one pours new wine into old wineskins. If he does, the wine will burst the skins, and both the wine and the wineskins will be ruined. No, he pours new wine into new wineskins" (Mark 2:22).

In 1992, the drugstore chain CVS discovered that only 7 percent of its 10,000+ workforce was over age 55. They conducted a study of their older employees and found that they were less likely to call in sick than the younger employees, and they were still capable of performing demanding tasks. Seventy-year-olds could still lift boxes and 90-year-olds could handle tough management jobs. So CVS began recruiting workers 55 and over, and today its older workforce has more than doubled to 16 percent of the total employee population. Older workers, CVS finds, need less training in areas like customer service, and they show high degrees of loyalty and dedication to their jobs.[1]

#3 CHOOSE THE ETERNAL OVER THE TEMPORAL

Paul said, "So we fix our eyes not on what is seen but on what is unseen, for what is seen is temporary but what is unseen is eternal" (2 Corinthians 4:18).

A wealthy young man asked Jesus want he had to do to have eternal life. Jesus told him to go and sell everything, give it to the poor and to follow Him. But the young man refused the offer—not because he had money, but because his money had him. In fact, Jesus told him he would have treasure in heaven. He lacked an eternal perspective. His definition of wealth was only earthly and not heavenly. (See Luke 18:18-24.)

I am convinced that one of the most basic tools needed for true success is an eternal perspective in a temporal world. The temporal world is time-bound and fading. It will not last. We need to balance time by eternity and live in such a way that we are making an eternal investment.

As World War II was drawing to a close, C.S. Lewis, British professor at Oxford, lectured to a group of students. He paused and asked the class, "How can you go to college and study literature when London is under siege?"

He then answered his own question. "We're always under siege. The real question then is, Will you spend your life dealing with the immediate or the eternal?"

#4 CHOOSE FOR YOURSELF

Don't let others make your choices for you. Don't surrender your personal freedom. God has made us free. America's greatest virtue is freedom. Freedom starts in the mind. We must think for ourselves—think things through; be a deep thinker. Don't accept the party lines and the media hype.

Spiritually, we have to move from inherited faith to integrated faith so that we can say, "I know whom I have believed and am persuaded that he (Jesus) is able to keep what I have committed to him against that day" (2 Timothy 1:12, *NKJV*).

When I was 7 years old, I committed my life to Christ. I used to ask my mother if I was a Christian. She replied, "David, only you can answer that question." Later, I made a profession of faith during a worship service. It was my personal choice—a choice that has shaped my life and destiny. I can honestly say, "I know whom I have believed."

David penned the timeless words, "The Lord is my shepherd." The key word is *my*. He, too, saw in personal terms.

#5 CHOOSE NOW—DON'T PROCRASTINATE

Every day God gives us the gift of time—24 hours, 1,440 minutes or 86,400 seconds. We can spend it, waste it, use it, but we can't save it. It passes quickly. The great enemy to using our time for the glory of God is the enemy of procrastination.

Procrastination comes from two Latin words, *pros* meaning "forward" and *cras* meaning "tomorrow." Mark Twain said, "Never put off until tomorrow what you can put off until the day after tomorrow."

One of my favorite Bible stories is about Pharaoh and the frogs. One day Pharaoh called for Moses after the second plague, the frogs, had come upon Egypt. The plagues were divine judgments against Pharaoh for his idolatry and harsh treatment of the Israelites. During the first plague, the Nile, regarded as the Father of Life, turned to blood. Pharaoh only hardened his heart. Then came the second plague—frogs. They were everywhere. So Pharaoh pleaded with Moses to pray to God and end the plague. Moses asked him, "When do you want the frogs removed?"

Pharaoh gave a ridiculous response, "Tomorrow." He might as well have said, "Give me one more night with the frogs." Here was a man with no sense of time.

#6 CHOOSE PATIENTLY

My mother was fond of the sayings, "Rome wasn't built in a day," and "Fools rush in where angels fear to tread." She said those things to me often, because I was so impatient and so impulsive. I'm the kind of person who would like patience, if I had the time to learn it! Yet, we all know that patience is a powerful virtue and an indispensable element in achieving success.

We need balance in this area. Some people rush into things impulsively without thinking them through. A woman in her late 30s was desperate to get married, so she went to a fortune teller to find out if and when she would meet Mr. Right. The fortune teller said, "You will be proposed to three times in the next year by three men."

"No, I won't," she replied, "because I'll accept the first one."

Stay away from the paralysis of analysis. Some people are forever analyzing without taking action. If God had given the work of creation to a committee, we would still be in the third day!

Keep your focus. You may have the right plan but can't stay on track. Keeping focus is crucial to achieving success. Many adults have ADD (attention deficit disorder). They get distracted and can't keep their attention on the goals. They have ACD (attention carrier disorder), or AMD (attention marriage disorder). The lack of staying power keeps people from their goals. We have to resist growing tired of the process so that we don't stop short of our goals.

These then are the enemies of patience we need to master: impulsiveness, the paralysis of analysis, the lack of focus and the loss of staying power.

#7 CHOOSE REPEATEDLY

Sometimes you have to make some choices over and over. It's important for married couples to renew their vows and commitment; to choose each other all over again. Sometimes this means going on a second honeymoon, a formal renewal of vows, or just making a conscious decision to choose your spouse again.

Joshua was not issuing a new charge but an old one when he said, "Choose for yourselves this day whom you will serve" (Joshua 24:15). Moses gave the same challenge before he died. Joshua was calling for covenant renewal.

Jesus led Peter in a renewal of his vows of faith and ministry. When Peter denied Christ, he gave up his calling and went back to his fishing business. But the risen Lord went to Peter at the Sea of Galilee. He asked him, "Do you love me?" Peter said, "Lord, you know I love You." Jesus told him, "Feed my sheep." He renewed his faith and his commitment by the waters of the Galilee and went back to fishing for men.

#8 CHOOSE COURAGEOUSLY

Choices require us, at times, to go against the tide of pubic opinion or against the masses. Jesus talked about two roads and the need to choose the right one courageously. It's easy to take the broad road and follow the crowd, but remember it can lead to destruction. Better to take the narrow road that leads to life. It takes courage to make the right decisions.

Robert Frost, penned these inspiring words in "The Road Not Taken:"

> *Two roads diverged in a wood*
> *And I took the one less traveled by*
> *And that has made all the difference.*

#9 CHOOSE DECISIVELY

Let's confront the myth of neutrality. Dante said, "The hottest places in hell are reserved for those who in times of crisis reserved their neutrality." Jesus said, "He who is not with me is against me and he who does not gather with me scatters" (Matthew 12:30). Elijah, the prophet, asked the people of his day, "How long will you waver between two opinions?" (1 Kings 18:21).

This holocaust statement appears on the wall of the Yad Vashem Holocaust Memorial in Jerusalem. It is attributed to Martin Niemoller, a German Protestant pastor who lived from 1892-1984.

First they came for the Communists. I was not a Communist so I said nothing.

Then they came for the Jews. I was not a Jew so I said nothing.

Then they came for the Trade Unionists. I was not a Unionist, so I said nothing.

Then they came for the Catholics. I was not a Catholic, so I said nothing.

Last of all they came for me; and there was no one left to speak.

#10 CHOOSE WHOLEHEARTEDLY

I believe in doing everything wholeheartedly. If it's worth doing, it's worth our best effort! Joshua challenged the people to get off the fence and make a stand to follow the Lord with all their hearts. Remember the words of Solomon: "Whatever your hand finds to do, do it will all your might, for in the grave where you are going there is neither working nor planning nor knowledge nor wisdom" (Ecclesiastes 9:10).

According to legend, a man was out walking in the desert at night when a voice said to him, "Pick up a handful of pebbles and put them in your pocket. Tomorrow you will be both sorry and glad."

The man obeyed. He stooped down and picked up a handful of pebbles and put them in his pocket. The next morning he reached into his pocket and found diamonds, rubies and emeralds. And he was both sorry and glad. Glad that he had taken some—sorry that he hadn't taken more.

Erma Bombeck said, "When I stand before God at the end of my life, I would hope that I would not have a single bit of talent left but could say, 'I used everything you gave me.'"

Endnotes

[1] Joe Mullich (26 Nov. 2003) "They Don't Retire Them, They Hire Them," *Workforce Management* <http://www.workforce.com>.

FINANCIAL FREEDOM

Did you know that the Bible contains some 500 verses on the subject of faith and about 500 verses on prayer, but 2,000 verses on the topic of money? Did you know that one out of every 10 verses in the Gospels deals with money and 16 of Jesus' 38 recorded parables concern money? Even Ecclesiastes says, "Money is the answer for everything" (10:19).

Obviously, money plays an important role in our lives. While money can't make us happy, the lack of it can make us very unhappy. Financial stress is reported to be the number one reason marriages fail. Our political elections are largely guided by economic forces. The advancement of the gospel and missionary endeavors rise and fall on financial resources.

God created us to be productive in every area of life—including our finances. God gives you to ability to produce wealth. The righteous person is like a tree, "whose leaf also shall not wither and whatever he does shall prosper" (Psalm 1:3, *NKJV*). The apostle John wrote, "Beloved, I pray that you may prosper in all things and be in health, just as your soul prospers" (3 John 2, *NKJV*).

On the other hand, we are cautioned against having the wrong attitudes toward wealth. Jesus said "the worries of this life, deceitfulness of wealth and the desires for other things" choke our lives spiritually (Mark 4:18). He also told us, "Be on your guard against all kinds of greed; a man's life does not consist in the abundance of his possession" (Luke 12:15). Remember, "The love of money is a root of all kinds of evil" (1 Timothy 6:10).

People have confused humble means with humility. Moses grew up in the wealth of Egypt, yet he was called the most humble of men (Numbers 12:3). Abraham had both great faith and great wealth. Job had enduring faith: he was the greatest man in the East (Job 1:3). Some people think Jesus was poor, but His father owned his own business and was able to afford rabbinical education for Jesus.

Jesus even had a treasurer for His ministry. Perhaps the gold, frankincense and myrrh given to Him at his birth by the Magi were invested to later underwrite His ministry. Jesus had several wealthy persons who supported His ministry: Matthew the tax collector, Zaccheus, Nicodemus, Joseph of Arimathea and Lazarus. Paul says for our sakes Jesus became "poor so that [we] through his poverty might become rich" (2 Corinthians 8:9). But the poverty spoken of here is not material but spiritual. He left the wealth of heaven to come to earth and the wealth He gives us is spiritual not material—the wealth of everlasting life which is the only lasting wealth!

Paul makes this clear in 2 Corinthians 9:6-11:

> Remember this: Whoever sows sparingly will also reap sparingly, and whoever sows generously will also reap generously. Each man should

give what he has decided in his heart to give, not reluctantly or under compulsion, for God loves a cheerful giver. And God is able to make all grace abound to you, so that in all things at all times, having all that you need, you will abound in every good work. As it is written: "He has scattered abroad his gifts to the poor; his righteousness endures forever." Now he who supplies seed to the sower and bread for food will also supply and increase your store of seed and will enlarge the harvest of your righteousness. You will be made rich in every way so that you can be generous on every occasion, and through us your generosity will result in thanksgiving to God.

While financial wealth is a wonderful blessing from God, there are even greater riches. In Scripture we read about the rich garments of righteousness (Zechariah 3:4), the riches of God's Word (Psalm 119:14), the riches of God's wisdom (Romans 11:33), being rich in generosity (2 Corinthians 8:2), the riches of God's grace (Ephesians 1:7), the riches of God's mercy (2:4), the riches of Christ in us (Colossians 1:27), the riches of spiritual understanding (2:2, 3), being rich in good deeds (1 Timothy 6:18) and being rich in faith (James 2:5).

I want to share with you 10 Biblical principles for financial freedom. What is financial freedom? Freedom from burdensome debt; freedom from worry, stress and anxiety about money matters; freedom from the love of money and the fear of poverty; freedom from greed and hoarding; freedom from secular thinking about wealth; and freedom from myths about money.

#1 THINK RIGHT ABOUT WEALTH

People aren't thinking right about money these days. For example, a lending institution advertises, "Now you can borrow enough money to get completely out of debt."

An Internet mortgage group advertises, "Now you can buy the house of your dreams with a mortgage of no money down and interest only." Interest only? That's thinking strange about money.

Your money management strategy will never be greater than the way you think about wealth. "As a man thinks . . . so is he" (Proverbs 23:7).

How do you see wealth? How do you define it? What are your inner values that govern the way you manage your money? Wealth means different things to different people. There are two major approaches to wealth that I have observed.

First, there is that larger camp of people who define wealth as the accumulation of things. They finance everything they can to enjoy things in the here and now. Since they define wealth as possessions, they are typically in a lot of debt in order to enjoy the good life. They have to obligate their time to work a lot in order to pay for everything, which is typically financed over long periods of time. The purpose of work is to produce wealth.

Second, there is that smaller group of people who define wealth as "freedom of movement." They build wealth so that they can do what they want to do when they want to do it. While wealth is the goal of the first group, this group uses wealth as a means to a greater goal—the freedom of movement. They want to be free from debt obligation so they can control their time.

The first group spends their time to get money. The second builds wealth in order to gain time. I can see only three noble uses for wealth:

- To enjoy life and bless your family

- To build long-term wealth for your family

- To advance the kingdom of God, which is the most important use of wealth.

A penny pincher was on his deathbed and asked to see his pastor, doctor and lawyer. "I have $90,000 under my mattress. At my funeral I want each of you to toss in an envelope containing $30,000 when you pass by my casket."

The day of the funeral came and each one passed by the casket at the viewing and dropped in the three envelopes. Later, they asked each other if they actually did as instructed. The doctor said, "I have to confess that I took out $10,000 for new equipment for my practice, but put in the rest." The pastor said, "I, too, need to confess. The church is in a building program, so I took out $20,000 but put in the rest." The lawyer said, "I am ashamed of you men. I deposited the check into my account and wrote a check for the full amount."

#2 SET PRIORITIES

Jesus said, "Where your treasure is, there will your heart be also" (Matthew 6:21). Our core values will determine how we make, spend, invest and give our money. Also, the way that we manage our money will have an impact on the condition of our hearts. Money follows the heart, and the hearts of individuals follow their money.

Jesus taught us to set priorities—decide what is most important and invest our wealth accordingly. "Seek first the kingdom of God" (Matthew 6:33, *NKJV*). Money needs to be invested in what is most important.

Ann Landers received a letter from a young father worried that his choice to put his family ahead of his career would cause them to ridicule him. A few weeks after that column appeared, Ann received several replies. Here is one: "My advice to people who think the fast track is the way to go: forget it. I chose that route and it hasn't made me or my family happy. The more money I make, the more we spend. It's a vicious cycle. I'm saddled with a huge mortgage and we do a lot of meaningless stuff to keep up appearances. If I had it to over again, I'd do it differently."[1]

#3 REMEMBER, ALL MONEY IS NOT THE SAME

Good money management starts with understanding that all money is not the same and, therefore, should not be used for the same purposes. God's money is not to be spent but given. Money for savings, investments and retirement should not be used for taking a vacation. Money needed for basic living expenses should not be squandered on hobbies and luxuries.

We would do well to use Monopoly money in our society. The different colored bills in the game help the players identify quickly the different designations. People often live in a state of financial confusion because they have their money all jumbled up, spending it without a master plan.

When Barbie and I taught our children about money, we gave them each three jars. When they received an allowance we had them put 10 percent in the giving jar, 10 percent in the savings jar, and 80 percent in the spending jar. The jars were visual reminders that all money is not the same. Keep the jars straight!

#4 GIVE GENEROUSLY

In John Bunyan's classic, *Pilgrim's Progress*, we read: "There was a man, some called him mad. The more he gave, the more he had." The greatest virtue of the Christian life is giving: "God so loved the world that He gave . . ." (John 3:16).

Giving is an act of worship. It takes time, which is a portion of one's life span, in order to work and produce wealth. When we invest financially in the work of the gospel of Christ we are, in effect, giving our lives for the gospel. God receives the time spent as the giving of our very lives to him. "Present your bodies a living sacrifice" (Romans 12:1).

I once read, "You write your autobiography in your checkbook." The way we give, reveals our spiritual priorities. "Honor the Lord with your wealth" (Proverbs 3:9). Are we honoring God for His goodness and grace by the way we give?

Giving creates a spiritual cycle of blessing. No one truly prospers until he or she starts giving. "Bring the whole tithe into the storehouse, that there may be food in my house. Test me in this," says the Lord Almighty, "and see if I will not throw open the floodgates of heaven and pour out so much blessing that you will not have room enough for it" (Malachi 3:10).

Jesus said in Luke 6:38: "Give, and it will be given to you. A good measure, pressed down, shaken together and running over, will be poured into your lap. For with the measure you use, it will be measured to you."

Paul tells us, "Remember this: Whoever sows sparingly will also reap sparingly and whoever sows generously will also reap generously . . . For God loves a cheerful giver" (2 Corinthians 9:6, 7).

There are three kinds of giving found in the Bible.

1. We are to tithe, which means to give the first tenth of our income. The word *tithe* means a tenth.

2. We are to give offerings of praise as we desire to give. Offerings are freewill expressions of thanksgiving to God. The people gave offerings during the time of Moses to build the Tabernacle (Exodus 25:1, 2). King David raised the funds for the building of the Temple by the giving of offerings (1 Chronicles 29:1-9). Mary of Bethany gave an offering of an expensive perfume to anoint Jesus in preparation for the cross. The cost of the anointing was about a year's income. Jesus said her extravagant worship would be commended in every generation (Matthew 26:6-13).

3. We are to give gifts to the poor. Poverty is a scourge on any society that needs to be healed. God's will is that "there should be no poor among you" but because of human sin and social struggles "there will always be poor people" (Deuteronomy 15:4, 11). We are to break the power of poverty and "maintain the rights of the poor" (Psalm 82:3). "He who is kind to the poor lends to the Lord, and he will reward him for what he has done" (Proverbs 19:17).

I watched a financial planner on public television give a motivational talk on how to become wealthy. He shocked the audience when he said, "The first principle you need to learn if you would be financially successful is to give away the first tenth of your income." This principle is called *tithing*. (The word *tithe* means a tenth.)

People ask a lot of questions about tithing. Here are the most common questions people ask and what the Bible says about the subject.

1. *What is tithing?* Tithing is a general principle, a basic guideline, of giving the first tenth of one's earned income for spiritual purposes and to support the ministry of the gospel of Christ.

2. *Why was tithing established?* In the Old Testament it supported the ministry of the priests, the Temple and the synagogues, and provided for education of children and help for the poor.

3. *Where should the tithe be given?* Primarily in the place of ministry where you receive the Word of God. We are to bring the tithe into the Lord's "storehouse" which at the time was the temple or synagogue.

4. *Should we tithe on the gross or net?* This is a matter of personal choice. The Bible does not address this issue since we live in a different economic system than the ancient world.

5. *Are Christians to tithe since it was part of the law?* Tithing predates the law of Moses. Abel, Abraham and Jacob gave the tenth of their wealth. Let me ask you: If the people under the law gave a tenth, should we who have the new covenant of grace be at least as generous as they were to support the gospel?

6. *Does God guarantee an exact hundred-fold return on every dollar given?* No, not in the sense of $100 for every one given. That is a distortion of what Jesus taught (see Mark 10:28-30). The hundred-fold return of which Jesus spoke was a metaphor to describe the abundance

of God in our lives at every level—spiritual, emotional, relational and physical. God will bless us in every way when we learn the power of giving to Him.

A minister sought to raise funds for a project at the church. On a Saturday night, he wired some of their pews with electrical circuits, and had control buttons inside the pulpit. The time came in the service for the pledges and he said, "Now I would like for you today to pledge to the Lord. How many of you would give $100?" He pushed a button and 25 people jumped up immediately. He said, "Praise the Lord, we are off to a good start."

Now, "How many of you folks will pledge $500 for the building program?" He pushed another button and 25 more people jumped their feet. "Hallelujah," he shouted, "we are going to reach our goal."

His final challenge came. "Who will pledge $1,000?" He pushed a third button and electrocuted 14 deacons!

#5 CONSERVE YOUR WEALTH

Spend wisely. Don't waste your resources. Stretch your money as far as it can go. Look out for impulse buying. Avoid the trap of consumerism and frivolous debt. Here are three major ways people are losing their money:

1. *Interest*: paying interest on consumer credit. Consumer credit usually means credit-card debt. Consumer debt is debt on an item that loses value, as opposed to something like real estate that increases in value over time.

Also, buying a house is typically a good investment, but home mortgages need to be properly evaluated.

When you purchase a home on a 30-year mortgage at around 8 percent, you will purchase the home at nearly three times its original cost. A 30-year mortgage can be reduced to 22 years by simply paying one extra payment per year. People lose their potential wealth each year by paying too much interest. The interest they spend today is their inheritance for tomorrow. Americans are financing their dreams down the tubes by living in debt and paying exorbitant interest rates on consumer loans and credit cards.

2. *Expenses:* Failing to discipline expenditures. When making a purchase don't ask, How much is the monthly payment? Ask, How much does it cost? Is the item worth the cost to you?

When Barbie and I were newly weds, we read Larry's Burkett's *Your Money In Changing Times.* We adopted his formula for buying things. Before making an expenditure, honesty ask yourself, "Is this item a need, a want or a desire?" We find that the formula still works.

3. *Boundaries:* Live within your means. If you want to discover financial peace, you need to develop an annual budget based on your net income, minus your tithe. The average American family spends 115 percent of their net annual income. Don't dig yourself a financial pit by living above your means. Better to have peace, than be in the pit of debt.

#6 LEARN THE PROPER USE OF DEBT

There is a difference between asset-building debt and consumer debt. We are hearing more today about getting out of debt than any time I remember. It used to be vogue to have debt. We were often advised to build credit through having debt.

The Christian principle is, "Let no debt remain outstanding," or literally, "Do not keep on owing anyone anything" (Romans 13:8). This verse does not forbid borrowing money. No where does Scripture forbid the responsible use of debt. Jesus told us to lend to those who want to borrow: "Do not turn away from the one who wants to borrow from you" (Matthew 5:42). Scripture only forbids not paying debts in a timely manner, failure to pay altogether, which is stealing, signing a contract we can't fulfill, and charging exorbitant interest rates (see Exodus 22:25-27; Nehemiah 5:1-11). Even Jesus advised the use of banks to earn interest on investments (Matthew 25:27).

However, debt should be used responsibly and paid on time. Avoid high interest rates and penalties. Know the difference between consumer debt and asset-building debt, such as a home mortgage. "Always show good faith," my mother taught us. My parents had large medical bills, which they had to pay slowly over years. But they always tithed and never hid from creditors.

Contact your creditors, explain your situation if you are having difficulty paying, and send them something every month to show good faith to retire your debts.

#7 INVEST INTENTIONALLY AND CONSISTENTLY

Jesus told this story to teach the power of investing intentionally and consistently.

> [The kingdom of heaven is] like a man going off on an extended trip. He called his servants together and delegated responsibilities. To one

he gave five thousand dollars, to another two thousand, to a third one thousand, depending on their abilities. Then he left. Right off, the first servant went to work and doubled his master's investment. The second did the same. But the man with the single thousand dug a hole and carefully buried his master's money. After a long absence, the master of those three servants came back and settled up with them. The one given five thousand dollars showed him how he had doubled his investment. His master commended him: "Good work! You did your job well. From now on be my partner." The servant with the two thousand showed how he also had doubled his master's investment. His master commended him: "Good work! You did your job well. From now on be my partner." The servant given one thousand said, "Master, I know you have high standards and hate careless ways, that you demand the best and make no allowances for error. I was afraid I might disappoint you, so I found a good hiding place and secured your money. Here it is, safe and sound down to the last cent." The master was furious. "That's a terrible way to live! It's criminal to live cautiously like that! If you knew I was after the best, why did you do less than the least? The least you could have done would have been to invest the sum with the bankers, where at least I would have gotten a little interest." Take the thousand and give it to the one who risked the most. And get rid of this 'play-it-safe' who won't go out on a limb. Throw him out into utter darkness" (Matthew 25:14-30, *The Message*).

Money grows slowly over time. In order to increase your wealth, you have to learn how to invest, not just live on earned income. Develop a lifelong strategy for building wealth. You have to be intentional with your money. Set specific goals and concrete objectives to reach those goals. It is important to get on the positive side of interest, so that your money is earning money.

Baron Rothschild, the financier, described compound interest as "the eighth wonder of the world." The first step in saving money is to stop losing it by paying exorbitant interest and undisciplined expenditures.

Consider "the rule of 72" formula: The number 72 divided by the compound rate of return equals the number of years money doubles. For example, at 6 percent return, it would double in 12 years; at 8 percent return, it will double in 9 years; at 10 percent return, it will double in 7.2 years.

Here's an example: A young person at age 22 graduates from college, invests $3,000 in a Roth account and leaves it there—no more investment. If the money gains an average annual return of 8 percent until age 65, the investment would be worth $92,500. Now, if this person invested $3,000 a year each year until age 65 at the 8 percent return, it would be worth $989,000!

God says, "My people are destroyed from lack of knowledge" (Hosea 4:6). Learn all you can about money management, sound investments and real estate. Ignorance is not bliss when it comes to making the most of your money. Think of money as a tool in your hand for the kingdom of God. Ask yourself how can I use my money to advance the kingdom of God and the gospel of Christ.

#8 BE CONTENT WITH WHAT YOU HAVE

When the Romans soldiers came to hear John the Baptist preach his message of repentance, they asked him what they needed to do to repent. He replied, "Be content with your pay" (Luke 3:14).

Some of you reading this right now, own your own business or manage employees and are going to put out a memo tomorrow at your company to all employees: "Memo from John the Baptist . . . be content with your pay."

I once read: "The happiest people don't necessarily have the best of everything. They just make the best of everything."

> Keep your lives free from the love of money and be content with what you have, because God has said, "Never will I leave you; never will I forsake you" (Hebrews 13:5).

Until you enjoy what you have, you won't be able to enjoy more. *Contentment* means, "not inclined to complain or desire something else; satisfied; submissive to circumstances; freedom from worry or unsatisfied desires." The difference between the contented person and the discontented person is not how much one has, but whether or not the person enjoys what he or she has.

Contentment does *not* mean to maintain the status quo, to settle for second best, or to turn down opportunities to better ourselves and our lifestyles. To the contrary, we are called to press on, to rise up to our potential and to accomplish great things for the glory of God. But we keep our ambitions in check as we experience a sense of fulfillment, peace and joy— regardless of our situation in life.

The contented person realizes the limitations of wealth.

Money can buy medicine, but it can't buy health and long life.

Money can buy tranquilizers, but it can't buy peace of mind.

Money can buy romance, but it can't buy love.

Money can buy entertainment, but it can't buy happiness.

Money can buy a meal, but it can't buy satisfaction.

Money can buy a house, but it can't buy a home.

Money can buy an education, but it can't buy wisdom.

Money can buy the good life, but it can't buy eternal life.

These things are gifts from God, bestowed on those who love and serve Him.

#9 ENJOY THE GOOD THINGS OF LIFE

Here's some sound advice from Ecclesiastes:

> "Then I realized that it is good and proper for a man to eat and drink, and to find satisfaction in his toilsome labor under the sun during the few days of life God has given him—for this is his lot. Moreover, when God gives any man wealth and possessions, and enables him to enjoy them, to accept his lot and be happy in his work—this is a gift of God. He seldom reflects on the days of his life, because God keeps him occupied with gladness of heart" (5:18-20).

He also said, "So I commend the enjoyment of life" (8:15).

We need to balance today and tomorrow. Some people are so focused on tomorrow that they fail to enjoy the moment. Wealth and time are meant to be enjoyed.

In my first pastorate, I counseled a young couple having problems. He was so obsessed with paying off the house in seven years, he wouldn't let his wife buy a new stove. I asked him, "How do you plan to eat in a few weeks when it goes out?" They didn't take vacations or buy new clothes because he was so obsessed. A few years ago when she died in a car accident, I preached her funeral. When I walked into the sanctuary and saw the family, my mind flashed back to that conversation we had many years earlier.

We never know how long we have each other, so we need to enjoy the things God gives us with the people we love. So, take that vacation. Buy your wife that piece of jewelry she's always wanted (if you can afford it). Get that something extra for your kids. Go out for that nice dinner, and get dessert!

Mark Twain said, "Twenty years from now you will be more disappointed by the things you didn't do than by the ones you did do."

#10 TRUST GOD TO BE YOUR PROVIDER

Let me tell you two truths about God. First, He owns it all. "The earth is the Lord's and everything in it" (Psalm 24:1). What a moment of liberty comes into a person's life when he or she relinquishes ownership. We are just managers of God's resources.

Second, God provides for His people. King David penned these powerful words: "I was young and now I am old, yet I have never seen the righteous forsaken or their children begging bread. They are always generous and lend freely; their children will be blessed" (Psalm 37:25, 26).

That's exactly what young John D. Rockefeller Sr. learned. Sure, he was a determined businessman who set out to earn his fortune. By age 33, he earned his first million dollars. By 43, he controlled the largest company in the world. By 53, he was the richest man in the world and the world's only billionaire. He then developed a strange disease (alopecia) where his hair fell out, his eyebrows and eyelashes disappeared and he was shrunken like a mummy. While his weekly income was $1 million, his diet consisted of milk and crackers. He was so hated in Pennsylvania that he maintained body guards. He couldn't sleep and all joy for living left him. The medical diagnosis predicted he would not live another year. The newspaper wrote his obituary in advance.

During those sleepless nights, he began to take stock of himself. He realized he could not take any of his money with him into the next world. One morning he awoke with a new resolve. He began giving his money to hospitals, research and missions work. He helped the poor and needy. He established the Rockefeller Foundation whose funding led to the discovery of penicillin, as well as cures for malaria, tuberculosis and diphtheria. He began to sleep again. Joy filled his heart. The symptoms began to disappear. Instead of dying at 54, as predicted, he lived to be 98. He discovered a great truth: "God loves a cheerful giver" (2 Corinthians 9:7). Giving gave him new life!

May God make you rich in every way, so that you can be generous on every occasion.

Endnotes

[1] Ann Landers, "Class of '73: There're Beamers and Smiling Beamers," *The Oregonian*, 26 Sept. 1991.